D0871026

REPUBLIC
OF
OUTSIDERS

Also by Alissa Quart

Branded: The Buying and Selling of Teenagers

Hothouse Kids: The Dilemma of the Gifted Child

REPUBLIC
OF
OUTSIDERS

THE POWER OF AMATEURS,
DREAMERS, AND REBELS

ALISSA QUART

THE NEW PRESS

NEW YORK
LONDON

© 2013 by Alissa Quart
All rights reserved.
No part of this book may be reproduced, in any form, without written permission
from the publisher.

Requests for permission to reproduce selections from this book should be mailed to
Permissions Department, The New Press, 38 Greene Street, New York, NY 10013.

Published in the United States by The New Press, New York, 2012
Distributed by Perseus Distribution

ISBN 978-1-59558-875-3 (hc)
ISBN 978-1-59558-894-4 (e-book)
CIP data available

The New Press was established in 1990 as a not-for-profit alternative to the large,
commercial publishing houses currently dominating the book publishing industry.
The New Press operates in the public interest rather than for private gain and is committed to publishing, in innovative ways, works of educational, cultural, and community value that are often deemed insufficiently profitable.

www.thenewpress.com

Book design and composition by Bookbright Media
This book was set in Goudy Oldstyle and Futura

Printed in the United States of America

10 9 8 7 6 5 4 3 2 1

To Barbara Koenig Quart and Cleo and Peter Maass

CONTENTS

INTRODUCTION

An artist who is also autistic argues for the value of thinking differently in a world that would rather cure her. A group of financial outsiders, sick of what they believe is a corrupt traditional financial system, are struggling to start their own bank. Cutting-edge scientists work to create artificial meat in labs, in the hopes of changing the lives of creatures around the planet. Bedroom rockers and micro music labels draw cult followings, never even dreaming of attracting major labels or reaching the Top 40. Film collectives and video sharers band together in spaces outside Hollywood's stranglehold. Bipolar people meet up around the country and are so ambitious about their own insanity that they claim the name Mad Pride. A new type of gender activist struggles against mainstream images of what it means to be female or male, and also the confines of gender itself. Crafters and urban farmers make or grow every shirt or vegetable they consume.

These are social outsiders and renegades who rethink what it really means to think differently. And they are just some of the amateurs, dreamers, and rebels who now compose an

America within America, making up what I call the Republic of Outsiders.

The rebels in this book are trying to live—and, sometimes, earn a living—outside the mainstream. They offer us alternatives by rejecting the dictates of convention. Using technology to dispense their cultural products or their ideas, they shake off the traditional constraints. While in the past being a social rebel—identifying as marginal or off-kilter or unprofessional—meant that it was unlikely you ever would reach wide audiences or change minds, the Internet has altered this equation, mostly for the better, though sometimes for worse. Today social rebels may try to bypass major manufacturers or conventional distributors. They may enjoy a more direct, more personal relationship with their audiences. They may reject outright typically distant, industrialized relationships between makers and users. Thanks to improved technology, they gather and organize much more easily now and turn their subcultural positions into strengths rather than weaknesses. These creative outsiders push up against the constraints—some legal, others more tacit—that society places upon them.

While all of these groups may seem at first to be disparate, they are all people on the fringes of American culture who are using similar mechanisms to get their messages, identities, ideas, or products to others like themselves and to the broader society. The people in this book represent not one sort of resistance but a continuum of rebellion. Yet all live out their beliefs and values more fully than many of us who tend to express our endorsement of difficult positions, identities, or causes simply by liking, Digg-ing, retweeting, donning plastic bracelets, or complaining in online comments.

Instead of relying on "likes" on Facebook, these outsiders work to create identities more authentic than those offered or imposed by mainstream society, in a process I call "identity innovation." These identities are often rooted in larger communities that act as a shield from and a challenge to the dominant culture.

Most of the people in this book share what I think of as post-identity politics—they are part of marginal groups united by chosen politics and tastes. Even the groups in this book who are initially outsiders by dint of more traditional identity markers—their mental illness, their gender nonconformity—now occupy specialized chosen niches such as Mad Pride or trans feminism.

More than forty years after "coolness" became a product heavily sold to American teenagers and then adults via blue jeans and rock 'n' roll, the people in this book represent a range of responses to the commercialization of, well, everything. Today, many acts of rebellion have become extremely elaborate negotiations with commercial culture. In a market-driven country where capitalism is all-consuming, most of the outsiders in this book respond to American entrepreneurialism with their own kind of cultural entrepreneurship. During a financial crisis, facing the inevitability of high unemployment and a contraction of the national economy, they often must piece together their own economic exchanges, as they have no other choice.

By innovating in this way, they are taking their lives into their own hands. We have long received our information, therapy, films, and even vegetables from authoritative sources: from insiders, trained or ordained to dispense this knowledge or cultural products. Most of the rebels in this book are changing that equation. They are proud amateurs who are doing for themselves and for others what only experts and professionals once did. They refuse simply to be a passive audience or designated consumers.

The traditional duality between insider and outsider has, to some extent, broken down. Media renegades, for instance, tend to be people who in a previous era would have been marginalized from established newspaper and media culture; now they create separate spheres where their voices are often more popular than the output of traditional news organizations. But then the most popular of these once-outsider voices are seemingly inevitably swallowed up by the big media brands. Or take a look at formerly fringe stances such as "animal protection," which has become so familiar that it's appropriated by burger franchises.

So what constitutes rebellion, originality, and resistance in a culture of remix? What is rebellious thought? In fact, what does it mean to be an outsider in a contemporary culture where "selling out" has almost become an honorific?

The results vary, of course. Sometimes rebels' attempts fail. Sometimes they succeed on their own terms. Whether these identity innovators fail or succeed, the outcomes can be attributed to the aggressively viral and short life span new ideas are now afforded in America. The line between the outsider and the establishment seems to shift by the day. Once upon a time, an established band or a musician disseminating music from her own small label was maverick or newsworthy; a few years later, that's closer to the industry standard. Some of the cases in the book, such as the once-disruptive technologies I first reported on years ago and considered for inclusion in these pages, including Craigslist and Pandora, have since become part of a new establishment. Craigslist radicalized sales and publishing, but sooner rather than later its owner had been recast as a kindly philanthropist whose site the *New York Times* dubbed stodgy and reactionary.

This trajectory isn't entirely surprising. In the last two generations, centrist culture in the United States has taken on and been enriched by novel, countercultural ideas, movements, and products, including civil rights, workplace safety laws, community antismoking campaigns, "green" architecture and cars, and the widening acceptance of gays (even in the military). And the digital has altered what's inside the categories "outsider," "indie culture," and "niche market": the Web has increased visibility at the margins because every rebel or amateur can publish or post his or her opinion. There is also a chance of anyone's output going viral. That in itself changes what is considered outsider or marginal and how "fringe culture" operates: alternative or subcultures no longer assume their messages are for the few or the like-minded. The idea of a mainstream is, at the very least, a useful cliché. Yet it becomes less of a cliché when we recognize that all cultures—the establishment culture included—are dynamic.

Of course, today's forces of rebellious style can also act as mere supplements to the mainstream. The stances, practices, or styles are often borrowed and watered down. Sometimes these outsiders are voluntarily co-opted, or what I call "self-co-opted," offered up to a more homogenous populace by the renegades themselves.

While the Internet has enabled saboteurs, it has also created an ephemeral culture where alternatives to the mainstream arise only to crash almost instantly or be absorbed into the established order overnight. Instead of a broad-based participatory democracy, digital culture has given us millions of fragments; while some offer a respite from the endless churn of late capitalism, the escape provided is usually fleeting.

This is not the first era in which this has occurred. Throughout history, movements, aesthetics, and disruptive technologies would eventually be formalized, institutionalized, and capitalized. Outsider styles would be borrowed by insiders and ultimately mainstreamed. Sociologist Philip Selznick popularized the word *co-optation* to describe this process when he wrote an analysis of the Tennessee Valley Authority's relationship with community groups and elites in the 1930s. For Selznick and others, co-optation is the process by which a dominant group copies or steals another group's ideas, style, or practices.

In his book *The Conquest of Cool*, Thomas Frank tracked the more recent history of this process. Frank wrote critically about how commoditization of "the alternative" was a hallmark of 1960s counterculture, which was quickly copied and neutralized by Madison Avenue as admen welcomed nonconformists as consumers. Frank further claimed that some advertisers presaged—and even triggered—youth rebellion.

More than ten years ago, when I was researching my first book, *Branded*, I also tracked the co-optation process, at a time when teen and tween girls' very identities were being invaded by niche marketing to an unprecedented degree: the teens themselves were being co-opted by large companies to market to one another. Scattered groups of teenagers and school officials tried to rebel in a process I called "unbranding," a complicated endeavor that often required its rebels to have a strong anticorporate style—a sort of renegade sales pitch—to combat soda sponsorship in the schools or reclaim public spaces where they could hang out. It was clear to me then and is even more apparent now that we live in a clever capitalist society that shapes our attempts to resist.

The rebels in this book take the tactics the "unbranded" teens and teachers used much further. But they also are more likely to try to take control of their own commoditization and achieve a truce with the mainstream, concocting novel ways of negotiating the straits. The aim for all of these outsiders, however, is to incarnate their authentic selves, while recognizing that spreading their ideas among "the normal" may require compromise. It's a type of co-optation that keeps us constrained by allowing us to loosen our strictures—but only slightly, within limits that keep dominant powers safe. While people do function outside of established institutions, there are plenty of conditions that limit or codify their activities. The self-co-opting tendency of some of today's outsiders has its limits: defining animal rights by "happy meats" at Whole Foods can be great, but it doesn't always lead to changes in policy or law.

For all the unlimited access of the digital age, there is also an upsweep of ignorance, mindless and sometimes dangerous outsiders, and irritating and self-promoting pranksters. Political theorist Jodi Dean has rightfully called our period one of "communicative capitalism": we converse and interface endlessly, but all the transferred information and data flow doesn't ensure that any tangible meaning gets through. Experts once had been defined, selected, and mediated by journalists and their institutions, but now soi-disant experts present their knowledge unmediated and out loud online. An "expert" can be an autism activist such as actress Jenny McCarthy, who insists that vaccines caused her son Evan's neurological disorder—a claim with near-zero support in scientific literature. Is this sort of communication meaningful or effective? Her main defense is the line "My science is Evan."

McCarthy's celebrity voice can define a debate, blotting out esteemed science writers who have repeatedly and completely debunked the antivaccine claims. An opinion page editor on a major metropolitan newspaper told me that when he assembled a group of bloggers to accompany the daily print page, he knew he was in trouble when one of them, a professed conservative, informed him, "I won't be consulting any mainstream sources for my facts. I don't trust them anymore. It's the bloggers for me." Other problematic outsiders include pseudo-outsider types such as the discredited graffiti artist Shepard Fairey or the founders and early adopters of dirty hacker paradises such as 4Chan; these are not the best this generation of alternos has embraced or produced.

Not all possible outsiders have made it into this book, of course. For example, the natural birth advocates and the lactivists whose once-renegade movement has succeeded—to the point that formula has become much harder to obtain in hospitals—aren't here. Neither are right-to-lifers, exemplars of the new American atheist movement, single parents, or married gay couples. Nor have I included many other outliers: the people I interviewed who were into DIY birth, having babies without anyone else on the premises; the gun stockpilers; the Northern California Zen visionaries; the low-calorie crowd seeking eternal life through near-starvation; the raw milk aficionados; the Tea Party; and even the freegans, clad in torn jeans, Dumpster-diving for discarded apples and pears. I got as many as I could on these pages, however. My goal wasn't to provide a comprehensive overview of modern rebellion but rather to investigate a series of examples.

By placing these seemingly unlike cases alongside one another, I saw better what they shared: stakes, goals, and practices.

In the middle of the nineteenth century, at a Woodstock-like convention—a sort of politicized proto–Burning Man—held in Rutland, Vermont, marginal or paradigm-shifting journalists exchanged their samizdat, blog-like journals. At the Rutland Reform Convention in 1858, these free-love advocates, ultra-abolitionists, vegans, and female atheists had their penny papers and free journals in support of their lost (and found) causes. They spread the word about the communities' then-radical outlooks and used their print platforms to criticize the government. In an age of rapid change due to industrialization, they espoused dozens of enlightened ideas, including the end of slavery. They also championed temperance, pacifism, mesmerism, and law reform. America has long been a country of cultural tribes, spread out and fragmented.

The country has been an incubator for the alternative viewpoints of those who wander off the predictable path, from the Transcendentalists to the hippies, from the Moderns to members of Esalen, from feminists to punks. Resistance embodied by these groups has taken many forms, from geographic self-isolation to distanced intellectual critique. And every generation has eventually found a home for at least a few subsets of individuals whose criticisms and opposition affected larger cultural trends.

This book is a portrait of some of these outsiders along with outsiders who are becoming insiders. The identity innovators in these pages occupy spaces where the broader society hadn't thought to or wouldn't deign to inhabit. They do so in the shadow of the abject failure of a number of established institutions. To my mind, they are radical extensions of the teenagers and teachers I encountered when writing *Branded* who were trying to fight back against advertising in their textbooks and corporate invasion of public space. Skeptical smart-set types may claim from time to time that there are no subcultures anymore. On the contrary, there are a seemingly infinite number—so many, in fact, that they are everywhere, challenging notions of outsider and insider.

When I went looking for the shape resistance might take as of 2012, Occupy Wall Street was still a prime example. In 2011, its motley brigades charged up the masses to describe wealth and power and an outsider majority with such catchphrases as "the 1 percent," "the 99 percent," and even the multiuse "Occupy." After the physical Occupy protests in New York City's Zuccotti Park were forcibly shut down in November 2011, many people continued the protest, organizing May Day actions and creating Occupy working groups of all kinds. One legacy of the movement may be linguistic, the language used to frame who is inside and who is outside: the "occupiers" are simultaneously marginal outsiders and, in terms of "percent," the vast majority of the citizenry, a sort of alternative entrepreneurialism where what is "sold" is an idea and a set of values rather than a pair of heels or a badge.

Nonprofessional enthusiasts are flourishing in an era when purported professionals—politicians, pundits, weapons inspectors, emergency relief agents—seem to fail us at every turn. The incompetence of these experts, from the Hurricane Katrina debacle of 2005 to the bank collapse and then the bailout of 2008, which led to an ongoing recession, not only has motivated amateurs to take matters into their own hands but also has, not coincidentally, become a common target of criticism for them. We are at a crossroads where it can seem like every mainstream institution is hurting us, from the too-big-to-fail banks to the lobbyist-saturated government and the laugh-track entertainment industry. Yet there's a silver lining in all of this, along the lines of Nikolai Chernyshevsky's purported remark "The worse, the better."

There is strength in the uncooked, the untrained, and even the unpaid. The people in this book often started on the outsider path when their trust in authority faltered and they fell back on their own intelligence to survive. They have created unusual, idiosyncratic identities in a superficial and financially damaged America. We can all learn from the new renegades and their unique ways of life.

PART ONE

OUTSIDER MENTALITY

1

BEYOND SANITY

I first met Sascha DuBrul when he was the only man in a little bookstore full of young feminists. He passed out postcards bearing the image of the Greek mythic hero Icarus. Within minutes of our meeting, unprompted, he showed me the tattoo on his back. I saw the image of a winged man, a black figure hovering over him. I didn't know that when he started to speak to me, I'd be part of a world that would include schizophrenics, an ashram in the Bahamas, and long-distance phone calls. He wore a sparkly belt and had splotchy, ruddy skin on the sort of face people used to call "sensitive": a scarred, pretty young man. His infrequently washed hair pointed in many different directions.

DuBrul's postcards were advertisements for an online mental health support group called the Icarus Project. Founded in 2002, the project had a website that stressed alternative self-definitions for those labeled bipolar or schizophrenic and also stressed an educated skepticism about the mental health system. What made the group singular was that it was entirely peer-run by those whom others would call—or who would call themselves—either insane or mad.

DuBrul himself, a leader of Icarus, is bipolar. An early crisis came when the radio in his dorm room in Portland, Oregon, started talking to him—even though it was turned off. He eventually was flown back to New York by his mother and taken to the Bellevue Hospital emergency room and then the psych ward at a hospital in upstate New York. After leaving the psych ward, he floated around the country for several years, jumping trains, living on the street, working on a farm. Even after years of leading Icarus, DuBrul continued the uprooted, interrupted life of the intermittently institutionalized; at one point he wound up in the psych unit of the Los Angeles County Jail, where he conversed with lightbulbs. When he recovered, DuBrul became a farmer, working land near the San Francisco Bay Area. He wrote journals well and copiously in a spidery hand. Among his traveling companions during this time was a young manic-depressive friend who, he said, eventually killed herself. Afterward, he wondered: would his friend's fate have been different had she had a group of peers who understood and supported her? In his mind, the answer was at least potentially yes—especially since "expertise" clearly had failed her. So DuBrul started Icarus with a friend, Jacks Ashley McNamara.

Icarus grew out of an anarchic Web culture in which labels and personal definitions of self were not immutable things, but, rather, changeable and elastic. Communities could come together quickly to help a member in need. The Icarus and Mad Priders' position is that mental health disorders might not be wholly unwanted conditions that need to be eradicated with drugs. The Icarus Project prefers to call mental health conditions such as bipolar disorder "dangerous gifts" rather than illnesses. These groups defended the right of even those labeled very sick to choose not to take their meds if they felt those meds were doing nothing or harming them—or even if they were simply tired of taking them. Members of Icarus thus called themselves "pro-choice" about meds. While some Icaristas (as they refer to themselves) took their meds, others refused them. They asked: Do people with these mental conditions really need to see themselves through a label? Will a psychiatrist or a specialist *really* be more helpful to a lifelong "mad" person than a loyal group of friends who understand his or her experience?

Icarus members were renegades when it came to both self and language. Like many outsiders today, they were trying to create a new language with which to describe their minds. They challenged the entire rationale behind diagnosis itself: did such diagnoses help in the end or simply box people in with labels and mislabels? They represented one of the key "rebel rules": outsiders can change the language people use to describe them and thereby change the mainstream a little.

Icarus started as a kind of DIY service provider. Eventually fifteen thousand or so people joined Icarus online. The site recorded visits from twenty thousand unique IP addresses every month. Here the Web showed its power to offer, at least virtually, a novel kind of public space, where people with like mindsets or needs connected. The group developed chapters in New York, the Bay Area, and Portland; several chapters were established at colleges or universities as well. They used slogans such as "Friends Make the Best Medicine." They questioned the definition of themselves as "diseased" to begin with. Mad Pride was sometimes the name they used for themselves, sometimes the slogan they rallied under.

To me, they were part of one of the more limit-testing rebel

spheres out there: DIY mental health. In the same way musicians were firing their managers and filmmakers were distributing their films outside the multiplex, the Mad Priders were using
the Web and banding together to help themselves, sometimes
refusing medication and even psychotherapy. What they were
doing resembled something more familiar, called intentional
peer counseling, when amateurs and fellow sufferers counsel one
another rather than simply being counseled or medicated by a
psychiatrist or a doctor.

But Icarus and its brethren were going further than that. They
were taking diagnosis and treatment away from the gatekeepers
and taking it upon themselves to define their own madness. Even
when members assented to expert diagnosis and treatment, they
often reshaped its form or meaning for themselves.

At the end of one of our New York meetings, DuBrul opened
a bottle of pills and tapped his daily dose of lithium carbonate
onto his palm. "I don't remember life without them," he said
with a shrug before swallowing the pills as we sat in a coffee
shop in winter Manhattan. He reminded me of the people I
had met and sometimes hung out with in New York City when
I was a teenager and in my twenties. He had an unwavering
gaze and an aggressive vulnerability, what Yeats called "passionate intensity," as if he wanted to live in an urban treehouse or
a squat with me as his favorite roommate, even though he had
just met me.

"Meds allow me to lead a normal lifestyle—to stay up late, to
travel. If I weren't taking them, I'd have to take way better care of
myself, and not eat sugar or drink," said DuBrul. "What lithium
does—check it out—it's like having lead weights on my feet. The
drug lets me fly as high as I want to without having to keep my-

self in check. I don't take drugs because I think I am sick, but because I have superpowers I need to control."

This claim was outsize, even grandiose. But it was part of how he, like so many of the rebels I met, revised his disability or outsider status into a kind of power. Help from insiders and experts was construed as necessary but irritating, a needed limit on their independent action and impulses. They permitted this kind of assistance because it helped them to be more efficient or simply survive, but they considered it an evil exigency.

In place of activist dogmatism, DuBrul emphasizes the Icarus Project's focus on changing cultural perceptions and helping members change their perceptions of themselves. They took on the way that terms such as *sick* and *healthy* are used today. Even the word *productive* was challenged: he rejected, at least partially, the perceived need to become better, more pliant workers. He asked why anyone should get a prepackaged identity through mental health diagnoses.

Twenty years ago, another Mad Pride activist, Will Hall, got depressed. He went to a psychiatrist, who prescribed Prozac. He had a manic reaction, an occasional side effect of the drug, perhaps stemming from the fact that he's bipolar—without mood stabilizers, Prozac has the potential to exacerbate mania. In his manic state, Hall lost his job at an environmental organization. He descended into poverty and started to hear furious voices in his head. He walked the streets of San Francisco night after night, but the voices never quieted. He got so desperate that he went to a clinic for help; he was swiftly locked up. He said he was diagnosed as schizophrenic, hospitalized, and placed in restraints against his will. Then his health insurance ran out. A social worker came and arranged his discharge. He wound up in a homeless shelter and went from there to group homes and programs. He eventually recovered a little, enough to begin asking whether the treatment he'd received was the most useful to him and other people like him, people he had met in clinics and hospitals.

On the surface, this story is about the fall of a promising young man into pain and out of the ordinary world. But in truth, Will Hall's history led him to become a renegade—and, in a way, to become truly himself. As soon as he was on his own, Hall began to imagine a different kind of treatment for people like him, people with extreme mental states and different ways of thinking. What if he had had someone like him counseling him at the hospital? What if he refused to see himself as a "broken invalid," as he has written, fearing "what was inside me as signs of my 'disorder'"? What if he refused to turn over authority of his mind and experience to doctors and therapists? He decided to throw himself into what is called "alternative mental health": avoiding milk, caffeine, and sugar; embracing yoga and exercise; watching his sleep patterns.

Hall started to read books about mental health and get involved in the budding online mental health scene, where people who called themselves "patient-survivors" met and chatted about their experiences. He wanted to find groups, online or off-, run by people with, as he put it, "severe mental illness labels" themselves. But when he couldn't find these communities outside the mental health system, Hall and a man named Oryx Cohen started their own such community, the Freedom Center, in 2001, with an Internet radio show and a weekly support group. He posted other people's stories of their recoveries on the center's website.

"We don't want to be normal," Hall proclaimed. Many say this, but Hall *really* meant it. Like DuBrul, he cut a striking figure: delicate and thin, with dark plum polish on his fingernails and black fashion sneakers on his feet, his mother's Native American ancestry evident in his dark hair and eyes. He was unusually energetic, seemingly vibrating even when sitting still. He spoke in a precise, scholarly tone, although I could hear a bass line of anger in his voice as well. The medical establishment, he said, has for too long relied on medication and repression of behavior of those deemed "not normal."

Throughout the 2000s, both Hall and DuBrul got better mentally, despite their schizoaffective and bipolar disorders. They led Icarus's growing constellations: the online and IRL ("in real life") meetings across the country, the other "mad people" they trained to help people like themselves avoid what they called forced drugging or hospitalization. Hall and DuBrul told people about prescription side effects and fought against what they called "drug overmedication."

Getting better did not mean the end of their challenges. DuBrul still struggled with manic episodes, when he might wind up half dressed on a roof in the middle of the night. Hall still occasionally believed plants were communicating with him. He found an alternative way of interpreting such contact, one that created a normative context in which it was not labeled evidence of insanity. Hearing voices, according to his mother's Native ancestors, was a sign not of madness but of an ability to communicate with the spirit world. He didn't think of himself as being antidrug, but he disliked the effect drugs had on him: what they did to his head and his personality, how they made him feel soft and slushy.

DuBrul and Hall offer an inspiring but also, to some, challenging model, not just for the mad but also for many of those considered "well." Some supposedly mentally healthy people take sleeping pills or go to couples therapy. Could they learn how to get to sleep without Ambien or take therapy into their own hands, talking with friends about the worst parts of their marriages? Should they? Although Mad Pride is not that widely known, the thinking behind it is increasingly part of a therapeutic counterculture: people who have gone off their psychoactive medications for garden-variety depression; those who remain wakeful but now lay off the sleeping pills, seeking to "go natural."

In the hopes of impacting both the "well" and the mentally ill, Icarus posts videos of its meetings on Vimeo and elsewhere to show members and interested parties how they work. In one video, "Icarus Project Peer Support, Part I—Checkins," a small group convenes in a book-lined room, and two co-leaders start off the discussion. The fact that two people share leadership suggests an effort to decenter the authority in the room, even as they explain the rules. One leader starts with the Meeting Agreements, ground rules for the discussion, "to make this a safer space for everyone and to make everyone feel a little more comfortable."

"Conflict is OK," says one leader. "It's how we learn and grow." Several of the rules acknowledge that there will be disagreement and divergent experience in the room and ask for attention and respect. The other leader encourages "'I' statements"—"I am hearing," "I am feeling"—by which attendees can let others know they hear and are reacting to what others say. The rules aspire to a group that is conscientious, aware, and careful.

Neither leader presents herself as an expert or an unimpeachable authority. Both are clear that rules are rules, but that everyone in the room is equal and deserves equal airtime and respect. (One of the rules is that people who talk a lot will be asked to listen, and those who don't talk much will be encouraged to speak.) The leaders are there to organize the discussion but not to establish hierarchies of knowledge or authenticity. Personal experience is what's authentic. There will be no middleman, no relay of fiat from on high. In this small room, for this small group, the ideal is a level playing field.

One night I spent with the Icaristas was at a party hosted by a psychologist. It was for the publication of a book of photographs of (what else?) a famous mental institution. DuBrul was clearly a star. Thin, with a dusty backpack and a shambolic walk, he gave tremendous embraces; he had a hint of the guru about him. DuBrul was surrounded by young Icarus Project members and was deep in his punk rock alter ego, whom he called "Sascha Scatter." At one point he spoke to the assembled shrinks, mentioning his own psychic struggles. He was applauded by these psychologists and analysts, who seemed eager to show their approval of patients as the prime movers in their own recovery.

PATIENTS LIKE ME

The diagnosis and prevalence of psychological disorders have increased dramatically in the past few decades: one in four American adults is said to have one, and the number of people taking medications for all of these newly diagnosed conditions has mushroomed. In 2011, the U.S. Centers for Disease Control studied the 2.7 billion drugs (this includes over-the-counter preparations and dietary supplements) that had been provided, prescribed, or continued during visits to doctors and hospitals in 2007.

Of those, 120.57 million were for antidepressants. Between

1995 and 2002, the use of antidepressants went up 48 percent. According to another statistic, between 1994 and 2003 the number of children and teenagers diagnosed as bipolar jumped fortyfold. From the mid-1990s through the late 2000s, the rate of antidepressant use went up 400 percent.

In such a social context, the Icarus Project railed against what it considered to be excessive medication and diagnosis. By constantly challenging authority on the basis (at least in part) of their superior knowledge of how they themselves have reacted to diagnosis and treatment, they were arrogating to themselves a kind of authority that competes with the medical establishment's.

Unlike older self-help groups such as Alcoholics Anonymous, the Icarus Project wasn't pushing a particular brand of self-help. Instead, they were pressing for both skepticism and community. On any given day, the Icaristas scurried around the group's purple-painted office, collating Mad Pride handouts and planning "mad awareness" events at colleges or universities.

They were ordinary people taking back control and treatment of their lives, ambitions, and conditions from experts. Other groups expanded beyond mental health, such as Patients Like Me, a website where people sign up, track their progress and status in terms of illness and treatments (in the most obsessive and detailed ways), and "subscribe" to one another to keep watch on one another's progress. The founders were Jeff Cole and James and Benjamin Heywood, two brothers who decided to build the resource when a third brother was diagnosed with Lou Gehrig's disease. (James eventually became the subject of *His Brother's Keeper*, a book by journalist Jonathan Weiner.) People with mental health conditions posted videos about their experiences to Patients Like Me. One showed a youngish, bespectacled woman, directing her commentary straight at the camera, somewhat awkwardly: "Hi, my name is Dana. I am not alone."

Her condition, bipolar disorder, she said, "is not me"; rather, "it's a part of me." It's not a badge, she said, not "a scarlet letter." In 2012, 172,752 people were using Patients Like Me. Among those on the site in that year, 12,277 had major depression and 9,761 had generalized anxiety disorder. One user in the mental health area of the site was a pink-haired stay-at-home mom who posted about her depression. Of course, like other sites of disintermediation, Patients Like Me can seem underregulated and potentially exploitative; not only is it a support network for people with shared illnesses, but it also mines and aggregates medical data for health care organizations and companies. (The benefit, however, is that as people with mental health troubles and conditions self-select and make their data available online, it could become far easier for researchers to study the efficacy of certain treatments.)

Carla Rabinowitz, a forty-nine-year-old peer-to-peer organizer for a community access group who is mentally ill and a self-described "mental health recipient," said the method is "so, so different than traditional psychiatric care. You see people like you who are thriving, people who are struggling. You see what you need to do to keep yourself going. I never ask for diagnoses; I have no idea what people's diagnoses are." She added hopefully, "A peer doesn't pathologize as much as a psychiatrist." Her organization prefers the idea of closing hospital wards and making community investments in hospital peer programs instead, under the premise that peer service is cheaper and better.

Icarus and Patients Like Me are encircled by many amateurs like Rabinowitz, including a long tail of other peer-to-peer organizers and thousands of mental health bloggers dedicated to helping themselves. Why should drug companies profit from treatments that the patients found ineffective? these Mad DIYers asked. Why should feelings be medicated? Why should they prefer treatment by professionals to help from friends and fellow sufferers? These activists were, like many of the other renegades I encountered, challenging authority and a "higher" class of expertise. In the Mad Priders' case, they were angry about drugs' side effects and aggressive pharmaceutical marketing. In the same spirit, bloggers and Icaristas repeatedly went after the anti-psychotic drug Zyprexa (olanzapine) because the drug's maker, Eli Lilly & Co., had marketed it off-label—selling it to unexpected demographics, such as elderly patients with Alzheimer's and other types of dementia—even though the onset of diabetes had been attributed to use of the drug in some cases. Bloggers helped expose the drug's ill effects. Along with the release of data on the rise of diabetes due to the use of the drug, the mainstream media picked up the patient-advocates' original investigating and reporting. Professional journalists started publishing pieces that questioned usage of the drug. Some of the claims against Zyprexa spurred a class action suit, and as of 2007, at least $1.2 billion had been paid for injuries sustained because of the drug.

But the Icaristas and people like them were not just interested in cause and effect. They were romantics of a sort, Web-fueled variations on earlier ideas of the outsider. "For the Outsider, the world is not rational, not orderly . . . truth must be told, chaos must be faced," wrote Colin Wilson in his 1956 book *The Outsider*, which not coincidentally was a bestseller. The book described the outsider as a nomad, a searching man who didn't fit into Society with a capital S—someone like the hero of the television show *The Fugitive* or Camus's *The Stranger*. Their version of the outsider, like the mid-1960s literary one Wilson embraced, tried to turn the stigma of exclusion, and also madness or transgression, into a kind of status, one with protective, alchemical properties.

Part of that romanticism was that DuBrul and Hall and their followers, as well as fellow travelers of the mind on mental health blogs, cast themselves as a human dam against a cascade of new diagnoses. Along with associated groups such as MindFreedom International (which advertised itself with slogans including "25 Years of Rethinking Psychiatry!" and "United Activism in Mental Health!"), Icaristas saw themselves as part of a small but hardy band who refused to accept the expansion of diagnoses such as bipolar disorder.

The more intellectual Mad Priders deem today's diagnostic trend to have a colonial cast: the more powerful class of the medical establishment and the pharmaceutical companies are cordoning off people who are "healthy" and calling them "sick" and thus in need of experts' intervention. They also argue for both public and self-acceptance of different minds. Hall said he hopes Icarus will "push the emergence of mental diversity. I am proud to be who I am and of my extreme states, no matter what the doctors say."

Unlike the mental health activists and self-help groups of the past, Icaristas aren't dogmatic; they don't prescribe a single lifestyle or set of beliefs. Using the diversity of the Internet, they embrace their own complex range of situations and positions on difficult issues such as medication or diagnostic labels. Whereas a dogmatic mental health activist might inveigh against taking any medication, DuBrul's style of activism accepts that not all medication is necessarily bad. The refusal to take medication, after all, wasn't what made them different.

The Icarus Project was a group that defined itself largely through writing. After all, Icarus characterized itself as aiming "to navigate the space between brilliance and madness." The name Icarus, drawn from the Greek myth of a boy who flew to great heights (brilliance) but then came too close to the sun (madness) and hurtled to his death, has an epic cast.

Not all of the Mad Priders had been professional psychiatric patients in the first place. At some point they probably accepted a severe diagnosis handed down in a frightening, one-way fashion that presented heavy medication as the only serious option. Like many, I had been struck by the haphazard quality of many diagnoses. I knew people who had pulled out their hair and thrown ceramic vases but who had never been labeled anything, and I also knew tempestuous but otherwise quite reliable folk who had been diagnosed with mental illness and institutionalized, often by their own parents when they were minors.

But there were other reasons the Mad Priders seemed more than just marginal outliers. Their mental states are, in many cases, seemingly only more extreme versions of the very recognizable mental states that fill ordinary lives. Between the proudly mad and what the dominant language calls normal there is a continuum rather than a break. As Adam Phillips wrote in *Going Sane*, "Madness may horrify us, but passion, strange eccentricity, careless and careful transgression" are all "the ingredients of modern individualism." In fact, the alt-mental-health movement began in earnest in the 1970s, when a number of activists who also were called mentally ill tried to organize an escape from psychiatry.

Judi Chamberlin, confined to a mental hospital in 1966

against her will and diagnosed as schizophrenic, is credited as the founder of the movement. She popularized the use of "Mad Pride" to describe a movement guaranteeing basic human rights to the mentally ill. When Chamberlin was a psychiatric patient, she discovered she had no legal rights. That moved her to co-found the Mental Patients Liberation Front. In her 1978 book *On Our Own: Patient-Controlled Alternatives to the Mental Health System*, she wrote, "That my depression might be telling me something about my own life was a possibility no one considered, including me." In the early 1970s, others in the movement followed Chamberlin's lead and fought for targeted deinstitutionalization of the mentally ill. That had mixed results, leading both to greater independence for the mentally ill and also to increased homelessness and incarceration of people suffering from these disorders when the promised community-based services to replace hospitals were not funded. Many patients were discharged not to pursue their liberation but to free the state of the obligation to care for them.

Another influence on today's Mad Pride movement came from the academy, which had explored new sociological and philosophical thinking about people with different mental states and their relation to society. In 1960, Thomas Szasz wrote that mental illness is a myth. In his most famous and most controversial book, *The Manufacture of Madness* (1970), he argued that insanity is just a word, one often misused to control uncommon, imaginative people. When I read one of Szasz's essays in 2009, I had flashes of other examples of this type of argument: Michel Foucault's famous writing on the history of madness and how institutionalized populations were subordinated, surveyed, and policed; and the work of the somewhat batty R.D. Laing, the antipsychiatry psychiatrist who questioned the validity of medical claims about mental illness.

More than two decades after Szasz and other academics and psychiatrists published their romantic theories of madness, a former mental patient named David Oaks, who had his first nervous breakdown while a student at Harvard College, co-founded the Mad Pride group MindFreedom, which extended beyond traditional psychiatry to include peer counseling. As with the Icarus Project, MindFreedom encouraged members to question the frequency and degree to which psychoactive medications were prescribed. And it brought peers—fellow madmen—into the psychiatric system as actors, rather than solely as people acted upon. After MindFreedom came such patient-run websites as Pendulum, bipolar groups on MySpace, and the extremely active site PsychCentral.

Now fifty-seven, Oaks helped create MindFreedom out of a coalition of thirteen groups; eighty-five groups with ten thousand members are now involved. It started with something called "Support-Ins" and a newsletter dedicated to what Oaks calls "psychiatric survivors," people who felt they have been abused by the mental health system. MindFreedom held counterconferences to the annual American Psychiatric Association meeting a number of times over the past twenty years to protest involuntary electroshock and other psychiatric practices. They also traded in a sort of cultural disobedience involving something they call "mad culture," which resembles many rebel cultures in that it celebrates the upside of being an outsider: the creativity and the otherworldly energies of the manic, for instance, or the intellectual honesty of the melancholic.

Mad Pride rediscovered the value of older programs such as

Soteria Houses (the word *soteria* is Greek for "rescue" or "salvation"), which began in Europe decades ago as places where groups of schizophrenics could live together in supportive, nonhospital-like communities. By dwelling in these communities for years, Soteria's schizophrenics had equivalent and occasionally better results, in terms of employment and social inclusion, than schizophrenics who received only medication. In the ideal Soteria House, people would have access to medication but would be encouraged to use it with great care, in a limited fashion, and often at dosages lower than generally prescribed.

Mad Priders also pointed to World Health Organization studies of developing nations in which psychoactive medications were not easily available. In such countries, people with schizophrenia were more likely to be employed and integrated into their communities than they are in Western societies. A study conducted in northern Finland also helped support the Mad Pride position by suggesting a conception of psychosis quite different from the one held in the United States: that it results from a breakdown in social relations rather than from a breakdown in the individual. The job of a psychiatrist or counselor is then to rebuild those connections. (More recently, Eli Lilly sponsored a study that claimed to debunk these findings.)

Bradley Lewis, a professor of psychiatry and humanities at New York University's Gallatin School, champions the Icarus Project and has brought its followers to NYU and celebrated their contributions through a conference partly devoted to their work. He sees Icarus as a Web-based "shadow" service provider, an extrastate element that steps in when health maintenance organizations, psychiatrists, neurologists, and medication fail. Psychiatry is sometimes faulted for devaluing the perspective of patients, defining them as just crazy—as nothing more than their illnesses. The Web and intentional peer groups such as Icarus have changed the equation, in many cases giving individuals more power over their treatment and fate. Amateurs now can preach a Mad Pride message and learn more about alternative therapies or narratives about mental health. If they believe a medication such as Zyprexa has hurt them, they can take action; find communities of like-minded activists; and, thanks to the reach and connectivity of the Internet, actually be heard. In Icarus chat rooms or on PsychCentral or MindFreedom, people who struggle with their states of mind can become masters of their own stories, instead of simply relying on psychiatrists to tell them what their stories are.

Of the early days of the Web, Philip Dawdy said, "Back when there were modems, you plugged your modems into alternative points of view about psychiatry for the first time." Dawdy, a sometime journalist who for eighteen years has called himself bipolar, was an omnipresent mental health blogger with the nom de blog Furious Seasons (his blog is now inactive). "For the first time, patients were educated about their own situation," he recalled. "So you were suddenly not totally dependent on the psychiatrist down the street, who is getting a $100 lunch from Eli Lilly."

Dawdy said he experienced a meaningful example of online intentional peer counseling on New Year's Eve 2004. He told me that on that night a seventeen-year-old boy posted the following on a MySpace bipolar group: "I want to kill myself." Dawdy said, "I spent three hours messaging back and forth with that kid, a perfect stranger, telling him not to, until he wrote, 'I am OK, I'm not going to kill myself.'"

The Icarus Project, explained Dawdy, was from the beginning composed of a lot of young people who, like that suicidal seventeen-year-old, almost got "sucked into the mental health system when they were fifteen or twenty-two, had nowhere else to turn, turned to people like Icarus, found a sense of themselves that's a lot more helpful than what they are being taught by their doctors. Icarus was for me when I was told I was in their situation."

To me, Icarus and the not-sane bloggers were also an example of what the theorist Michael Warner calls "counterpublics." Warner's term can be used to describe both the neurodiverse and many of the other renegades in this book who frequently turn to writing as a tool for expression and resistance. He sees these groups as creating their own fictions to counter the supreme fiction of the majority group, which never is the true monolith so many imagine it to be. According to his theory, what we usually call the public sphere is based on exclusion, and excluded groups are assigned lesser status. "Counterpublics" attempt to correct this, Warner says. The notion of a "public" is a social fiction, the "normal," and it becomes the frame for our lives. Counterpublics, such as the Mad Priders and all the others in this book, carve out separate spaces through writing in particular, through a strong message that people in the broader public may not have heard before and that could potentially change and shape minds.

As counterpublics define themselves through the act of writing, their presence and impact have never been more ubiquitous than they are in 2013. Autism bloggers, for instance, use written language to assert, define, and put forward their outsider opinions. They create public communities now through writing and publishing—self-publishing is, in a way, publishing a self.

While questioning the necessity of some psychoactive medications may seem to be the most shocking and irrational part of their stance—the truly outlaw aspect of their outsider movement—a range of evidence shows that this stance is far from crazy. Science does prove that drugs can reduce psychological distress, and some people do stabilize on meds. But not all do, and drugs can also worsen people's lives by giving rise to side effects ranging from impotence, diabetes, and obesity to more abstract complaints, such as a tamped-down emotional life or affect.

In addition, the advent of a wide range of new diagnoses, and the new treatments that go with them, has not necessarily led to greater functionality for those being treated. As journalist Robert Whitaker, author of *Anatomy of an Epidemic*, has written, less than 30 percent of patients recover and return to work, down from 85 percent in the pre-pharmacotherapy era. Though labeling and medication can be great tools when used selectively, in the case of manic depression the diagnoses have proliferated faster than YouTube videos.

Bipolar disorder used to be quite rare: just one in three thousand people was termed manic-depressive in the middle of the last century. Now an estimated two million Americans are told they suffer from some version of the condition. Various circumstances add to the frequency of the diagnosis. For example, some depressed people have a manic experience when exposed to an antidepressant (as Will Hall did) and may subsequently be diagnosed as bipolar when they are simply reacting to a drug or, in his case, are schizoaffective instead. That leads to a small inflation in bipolar diagnoses. In the past ten years, a new pharmaceutical market has been created for bipolar medication, alongside the rise in diagnoses of this condition.

These new diagnoses have flowered at a time when the *Diagnostic and Statistic Manual of Mental Disorders*, the diagnostic manual used by psychiatrists and psychologists, is often followed zealously and absolutely. Successive editions of the *DSM*—the forthcoming 2013 edition will be *DSM-5*—have tended to expand the definitions of many major diagnoses. It is in this climate that the Mad Prider feels particularly necessary. A few years ago, the psychiatric community started to question whether people diagnosed as schizophrenic should always use medications. The Icarus Project was ready and began talking to newspapers.

The Icarus Project, MindFreedom, and other Mad Priders argue that the emphasis in a new, closer-to-ideal mental health care model would rely on creating community and offering the peer services that can help define that community. And there have been strides toward such a goal. A new independent organization, the National Coalition for Mental Health Recovery, has a lobbyist dedicated to fighting for peer-delivered services for the mentally ill (admittedly, one is a lonely number compared to the legion of pharmaceutical lobbyists out there).

MindFreedom's Oaks called peer counseling the "solar power of mental health" and added, "We can't hire enough psychiatrists to support people." He dreamed of a day when, at any time of day or night, anyone in need could go online or Skype a peer counselor. There would be a single, united peer-to-peer online mental health service network. People could talk with a sympathetic, knowledgeable stranger "during a dark night of the soul." "It would be the very opposite of Chatroulette," said Oaks.

NOT WELL

Mental health activism such as DuBrul's and Hall's raises challenging ethical issues. There is risk here, real danger—an element largely absent from the alternative communities organized around cultural products such as music or film or around food or commerce. In *this* community of renegades, the cultural product is the self. Any challenge to its construction, any challenge to the mainstream's ways of defining the self, labeling "defective" selves and treating or restraining them, invites a certain degree of threat to both community and self.

There also is a risk that those in this community will hurt others or themselves. After all, people have committed suicide after stopping or tapering down their medication against medical advice. And researchers have found that in people with schizophrenia, there is a connection between the use of illegal drugs and a rise in the incidence of violent acts (although only a minority of schizophrenics are ever violent). In addition, people with schizophrenia who exhibited past violence and failed to comply with medicines also ran an increased risk of violent acts. If they weren't careful, these renegades might endanger themselves or others, I thought. Shouldn't Hall be controlling his thoughts with medication so that his plants could sit silently on the windowsill? Shouldn't DuBrul stop romanticizing a condition that still left him standing on the rooftops of buildings at night? It was another paradox of the renegade, a sign of the productive but often potentially dangerous elements of the Web-enabled outsider.

Indeed, conventional mental health advocacy groups do not accept alt-mental-health groups such as Icarus and Mad Pride. They warn against the uncertainty and instability inherent in having outsider DIY communities depend on their friends and allies on the Web, rather than on credentialed professionals. The charge is that people in the alt community deny themselves adequate care or downplay the seriousness of the neurological or psychological conditions others suffer. John Stanley is a founding board member of the Treatment Advocacy Center, a well-known organization for the mentally ill, and suffers from bipolar illness with psychotic features. He told me that "medication is indispensable for the majority" of people with bipolar disorder or schizophrenia, and he is very critical of "some of the views held in the [Mad Pride] community." Conversely, many in Mad Pride and Icarus would object to the Treatment Advocacy Center's support of "forced treatment" when deemed necessary.

Peter Kramer, author of *Against Depression* and *Listening to Prozac*, said that while he remains critical of the frequency with which drugs such as Prozac are prescribed and the too-wide range of situations for which it is prescribed, he isn't altogether willing to support members of Icarus who refuse to see their depression as a disease. "Psychotic depression is a disease and has been for most of human history," he said, arguing that, in most cases, depression is not productive or creative, just stagnant and disabling. Still, Kramer conceded that community support has an important place: "In an ideal world, you'd want good peer support like Icarus—for people to speak up for what's right for them and have access to resources—and also medication and deep brain stimulation." Some people diagnosed as mentally ill are genuinely unable to care for themselves. After receiving treatment, some formerly homeless people say psychosis drove them to live on the street and that diagnoses and treatment were their only ways out. The term *insanity* was a useful one for them because it got them the services they needed, however flawed.

Emily Martin, an anthropologist at New York University and the author of *Bipolar Expeditions* (Martin has bipolar disorder herself), explained, "The Icarus Project wants to valorize that condition—the close-to-the-sun metaphor of Icarus." She continued, "This goes back a long way—the celebration of the bipolar condition as a sign or a manifestation of a creativity we'd all be happy to have, with CEOs and actors who are said to be bipolar, or Virgin's Richard Branson. It's a condition packaged with ability."

While Martin was critical of the rosy grandeur of this perspective on mental illness, she saw real value in the patient activism and peer-to-peer help that could sometimes go along with that stance.

MAD LOVE

One night I had dinner with eight Icarus members, including DuBrul and Hall, at a Thai restaurant in midtown Manhattan. Over Singha beer, they joked about an imaginary psychoactive medication called Sustain, meant to cure "activist burnout." A bottle of red and black placebos that one of the members had created as a joke was passed around, to peals of laughter.

During that dinner, it was hard to imagine that DuBrul and Hall had been in a number of mental hospitals, although Hall was certainly distant—he had a certain cool glassiness as he checked his cell phone while other people were speaking. The bipolar Icaristas attributed this to his schizophrenia, but it could have just been the familiar alienation of someone constantly using a BlackBerry or iPhone—something that is also, of course, the province of "normal" people. (Between the bipolar and the schizophrenic members of the group, there was a narcissism of small differences.)

Another founding member of Icarus, a musician named

Madigan Shive, talked about how her mother had had psychotic episodes that led her to hoard. In her telling, her mother needed not only treatment but also a like-minded community that she lacked.

Shive spoke of how the "activism survivor movement" had saved her from what she called "psychiatric consumerism." "They've given me new labels and a new language," she said, gesturing at her friends. "I heard voices, but they were peaceful voices that told me intuitive things." When she was desperate she called or e-mailed the other Mad Priders, she said, and they helped her carry on.

While they sat in the restaurant, joking and planning speaking engagements around the country—they would travel together via bus to campuses to talk about their experiences—it was a demonstration of how small groups of renegades could, no matter how provisionally and how temporarily, relabel their experiences. While these "mad" allies were still clearly outsiders, they and the neurodiversity activists had taken their isolation and their suffering and created from it an all-too-rare thing: a community.

"We also want to be conscious that there are lots of contradictions," DuBrul told me at dinner. "I think pharma is evil, but the drugs are helping folks. There are people taking drugs who are ashamed to talk about it." He also told me that same night, "I've been in so much pain. That's why I want to find the kids like me when I was eighteen. I want to tell them that they're not alone."

A year and a half later, I talked to Hall again. He was off medication because he felt the meds had made his thoughts "slurry" but still lived independently, in an apartment with a roommate.

He had both girlfriends and boyfriends and maintained a large number of friendships, although they were often tumultuous. He lived in Portland, Oregon, studying for a master's degree in psychology at the Process Work Institute, a psychotherapy- and body-work-focused institution. All this had happened, he believed, because he had had support groups that enabled him to talk freely about his altered states as well as his everyday triumphs and struggles.

"For most people, it used to be 'Mental illness is a disease— here is a pill you take for it,'" said Hall. "Now that's breaking down." Yet his new way of handling his states of being didn't quiet the voices or the figures, like devils in Renaissance paintings, that still tugged at his mind.

But outcomes are complex. The alt-mental-health crusaders are great metaphors for all of today's social renegades both in their self-sufficient amateurism and in their ability to actually shock and surprise. (As Phillips wrote in *Going Sane*, "The sane can, in the fullest sense, get on with people; the mad are difficult.")

Nevertheless, the Icaristas and the Mad Pride people, buzzing and chatting online and weaving together their dissent, suggest that our trust in psychiatric labels—a central feature of modern times, when diagnoses are crucial for so many to get access to social services or even appropriate schooling—can cause unneeded suffering and lead to lifetimes of frustration and despair. Like DuBrul and Hall, many struggle with the way labels flatten us, whether the word is *gifted* or *inattentive* or *depressed* or *crazy*. In an age of labels, the Mad Priders have exerted their revenge against the vise of the "mentally ill" diagnosis, easing it open.

At their tenth-anniversary event in Manhattan in 2012, fifty

Icaristas milled about a borrowed meeting space by the Hudson River. DuBrul greeted me near the door with a huge embrace. He now lived in Berkeley, California, where he worked as a gardener and hung out with his friends who had kids, he said. He was stable, thanks in part to a new therapist, he said. At the event, older people mixed with college students. There was a three-year-old in attendance and also a woman in a wheelchair. Easygoing young women meshed with mad people who seemed a little closer to the edge. (DuBrul called the latter group "old-school patient-survivors.") In one corner, there were publications for sale with defiant titles such as *Cunt Coloring Book.*

After twilight fell, members of the group started to address the audience, five minutes at a time, in a fashion that resembled Occupy Wall Street's general assemblies—not entirely coincidentally, as their memberships overlapped. DuBrul cheered the group's ten years of existence, saying that they must have been doing "something right," but he was also startlingly honest about the group's challenges. "People find it [Mad Pride] when they are in a state of crisis or when their friends are," he said. "When they are better, they leave. We have fifteen thousand members on our website, but who holds shit down at Icarus?"

The speaker after him noted that the members who tended to hold things together in the group were the depressives. The bipolar types would have all the plans, and the depressives would then muster enough focus to carry them out, she said. The whole crowd laughed in self-recognition.

It was not a traditional triumphal anniversary event, but the Mad Priders seemed to feel safe in its unblinking honesty. They were yet again turning to the "expertise" of another former or current patient willing to listen and advise. They found community to be the antidote because they need an alternative sphere—a place where they are understood and a unique service that can't be simply bought or ingested. As the Icarus Project mantra had it, friends are the best medicine.

2

BEYOND FEMINISM

On a rainy fall day four years ago, a college freshman named Rey showed me the new tattoo on his arm. It commemorated his five-hundred-mile hike through the El Camino De Santiago in Spain the previous summer, which also happened to be, he said, the last time he felt free and happy.

We sat together in his room for a while talking. His tattoo resembled thorns and was of a piece with his spiky brown hair, tribal earrings, and baggy jeans. He showed me a photo of himself and his girlfriend kissing, his small drum kit, a bass guitar that lay next to his rumpled clothes and towels and empty bottles of green tea (one full of dried flowers), and the ink self-portraits and drawings of female nudes he had tacked to the walls. Thick jasmine incense competed with his cigarette smoke. He changed the music on his laptop with the melancholy, slightly startled air of a college boy on his own for the first time.

But Rey's story had uncommon dimensions. The elite college he first attended happened to be a women's school in New York City, Barnard College. When Rey, now twenty years old, first entered the freshman class, he was still legally female.

During his first year at Barnard, becoming a man was quite a challenge for Rey—not just because gender transformation, especially in one so young, could make people uneasy, but also because he was attending a women's college. His two roommates—"girly girls," he called them—had complained to the college's first-year housing director about being asked to share their rooms with a man. They wanted Rey to find somewhere else to live. They were disturbed when he told them on the first day they met that he was a transboy and wanted to be referred to by male pronouns. As he saw it, he was simply shut out by his roommates—and by the rest of the school. A week after learning of his roommates' disapproval, Rey, together with the dean and his parents, decided he should transfer to Columbia College, Barnard's co-ed affiliate.

Rey moved to Columbia for his schooling but still felt lost. The story of his rooming travails at Barnard ultimately wound up on the gossip pages of the *New York Post*, which cast him as an infiltrator in one of the last girls-with-pearls bastions under the mocking headline "Girly Gripe."

Rey was like other young people who saw themselves as "gender-fluid" and who were acting on that identity or those yearnings at younger and younger ages. They also were creating a new set of goals and a new language around their shifting personae and a large online community of like-minded people around themselves. Rey thought of himself as a *trans feminist*: he was interested in female spaces, from women's colleges and groups to all-women concert spaces, places where "genderqueer" people such as himself could find a home. Rey and other transmen and transwomen I met used a new language to describe themselves; one such term was *gender-nonconforming*. The more conversations I had with Rey and genderqueer people like him, the more I learned that after they transitioned they might well continue to refuse the neat boxes of gender identity—sometimes with emotional and intellectual seriousness, and sometimes with near-adolescent élan and bravado. Some wanted to live between (or among) genders. Some transmen wanted to be men, chemically or surgically or both. Some had had what is called "top" surgery or chest reconstruction surgery—basically a double mastectomy and reconstruction of pectorals, so that their torsos more closely matched the masculine ideal. Others didn't bother with any surgery or chemicals. One transman I spoke with got so comfortable with editing and reediting his gender that he stopped taking testosterone (or T, as it is called), the male hormone that makes voices deepen and facial and body hair grow. Ten years after becoming a transgender activist, he was now one of the gender renegades who dwell in the gray areas of identity: he painted his toenails and lived as a man who had married his female partner, a lawyer he has been with since attending the women's college Smith—a union that might have been illegal in some states if he were still defined as female.

Gender-nonconforming people compose an estimated 0.3 percent to 1 percent of the U.S. population. An April 2011 study done at the University of California, Los Angeles, found that 0.3 percent of American adults identify as transgender, or about 700,000 people. As no national data on this population exist, Gary Gates, a demographer at UCLA's Williams Institute, a gender-identity law and public policy research group, relied on two studies by state agencies to obtain that figure.

Genny Beemyn, director of the Stonewall Center at the University of Massachusetts, Amherst, has studied trans students on college campuses and said that people are transitioning earlier than ever. In order to accommodate those numbers, nearly five hundred colleges and universities nationwide now include gender identity and expression in their nondiscrimination policies, and the number is growing. (Students on campus sometimes use gender-neutral pronouns such as *ze* and *hir*.)

At one time, Americans who transitioned their gender did so in later, mature adulthood, but no more. David Valentine, an anthropologist at the University of Minnesota who studies transgender culture, was startled by the number of very young transpeople he had encountered in the past ten years. He said he never would have foreseen such a trend in the previous decade.

A good number of the gender-fluid, genderqueer transwomen and transmen I met called themselves by a name that particularly engaged me, as a biological woman and self-defined feminist: *trans feminist*, one of the terms Rey used to identify himself.

TRANS FEMINISM 101

What makes trans feminism different from mainstream feminism?

Feminism, of course, has historically been devoted to redefining what a woman can be, rather than questioning gender itself. The goal has long been to get women to claim and then achieve their professional ambitions and their professional places; in earlier decades; to stop women from suffering the constant sexualization or paternalistic protection of their bodies, and to gender-desegregate sports teams and help-wanted ads, among other arenas. Gender rights—women's rights—meant basic social rights, such as the right to equal pay for equal work or the ability to choose a future different from just getting married and having kids.

In the case of Rey and other gender-fluid students I met with who were attending Smith College or Mount Holyoke in 2008, trans feminism meant, in part, giving would-be students the right to apply to a women's institution as a "gender-neutral" person or to keep attending a women's college if they were transitioning to become men. Rey wasn't interested in just transitioning, though. He wanted to be an open transman and hoped to stay a feminist who still identified with the political and personal tribulations of his female friends and lovers after he transitioned. So did another trans college student I met who attended a women's college and lived in the campus feminist co-op. His nickname was "Harry Potter" because he looked like the actor Daniel Radcliffe in the movie series: thin, with metal-rimmed glasses, bowl-cut hair, pale skin, and bright blue eyes. He wasn't fully "out" to his parents because they had always tended to be very judgmental of him even before his testosterone therapy or his surgery. He said he still thought he had more "in common with women" than with men "because of the shared experience" of having been a woman all those years.

I met students who saw themselves as simply living on the gender continuum—not quite male and not quite female. One gender-nonconforming student activist at a women's college told me, "I find pronouns cumbersome and self-limiting." These individuals took no hormones and had no plans to have an operation to alter their gender; they were born female. Despite their resistance to gender pronouns, they were proud to call themselves feminists.

For transwoman Jesse Thiessen, a writer, being a trans feminist meant that after relinquishing the power of being a "straight white man for being a transgender lesbian woman," she would dress "like I like to dress," meaning that her clothes were often unisex (hoodie, sneakers) rather than superfeminine. "I didn't go through all this, the hormones and the rest," she said, "to become someone else's idea of a woman."

In the late 1990s, the term trans feminist, credited to Diana Courvant and Emi Koyama, was applied to a coalition of transgender people and feminists. The argument was that both biological women and trans women dealt with the oppression of women. Both groups also struggle with distorted female body images and female-specific health concerns.

Julia Serano is a trans feminist author whose work these college students were reading. She lives in Oakland, California, and every now and then over the past four years I'd check in with her. A blond, ponytailed forty-five-year-old biologist, she wrote a well-received memoir about her own struggles as a transwoman, *Whipping Girl*. She transitioned ten years ago, although she had been thinking about changing her gender for much longer than that. Twenty-five years ago, she could find only "bad psychology books" about gender confusion, she tells me. She would read these books in secret during her college years. For Serano, trans feminism became a major force in her life after she transitioned.

Lawyer and transgender legal scholar Dean Spade put it to me this way: "If you are identified as female, you will still have trouble being accepted as a firefighter. Liberatory movements"—such as trans feminism—"are trying to reduce the gender norms, that boys and girls have to walk one way or another or that men and women have to have sex one way or another."

In 2012, Serano was involved in online debates on the feminist magazine *Ms.*'s website about *Ms.* blogger Aviva Dove-Viebahn's post titled "Future of Feminism: Transfeminism and Its Conundrums." Dove-Viebahn called transgender issues a "sticking point" in feminist circles. Serano felt the writer had "framed trans feminism as a controversial and debatable submovement within feminism." Serano instead defined it as a movement to assist "anyone who fails to conform to the gender binary—whether an intersex child, a tomboyish girl, a gay man, a transgender person, etc.," and pointed out that these people are all marginalized by society. "The gender binary concept was an attempt to create a synthesis between feminism, queer and transgender activism." As she put it, the gender binary, or the clear division between men and women with nothing in between, is "a system that oppresses trans people and -women and -men more generally." Trans feminists look at things "intersectionally" or read women's rights through the lens of race, class, and transgender rights as well, said Serano. For example, considering feminine males to be lesser men, she writes, is another kind of sexism that she dubs "effemimania" and believes is an underexamined social toxin that trans feminists should take on.

In my conversations with Serano she was always a sprightly sounding optimist, and I felt I easily understood where she was coming from. After all, I had come of age as a feminist in the 1990s, *the* moment of "third-wave feminism." ("Always put 'third-wave feminism' in quotes," Serano chortled.) The so-called third wave tried to make feminism more pluralistic and to take in a lot of voices that had been excluded or not accounted for in the American feminism of the 1960s and 1970s. Serano saw trans feminism as a kind of final stage in that evolution, where women join with gender-fluid people and transwomen and -men to recognize that transphobia often shares a lot with sexism against biological women.

Trans feminism meant that women's institutions must rethink their ideas of gender, as Barnard was asked to do with Rey, as well as greater acceptance of transmen in women's spaces and institutional accommodations for people who are genderqueer.

When people say transwomen "are too feminine—insincere and manipulative—these people are critiquing the properties of femininity as much as they are critiquing the transwomen," said Serano. "After all, I was teased and bullied for my feminine tendencies before I transitioned." She wondered if there could be a larger movement that unites femme-y people—effeminate men, feminine women, butch women, *and* gender-fluid people of all stripes—against their joint oppressors.

When I asked Serano for concrete examples of pushback against her movement within feminism as a whole, she mentioned the debate over whether women should stay at home with children. "There are assumptions in this debate: that all women want to have children or are able to, or all women can adopt children," she explained. "But who is left out of that?" A funnier, wilder example of how trans feminists don't always fit into feminism overall can be found in one of Serano's 2012 tweets, at a time when women's rights to contraception were again threatened: "But I have to say that as an infertile woman, all this contraception-centric feminism over the last month has been alienating for me."

I wondered at Serano's cheeriness. After all, trans feminism seems to be somewhat ignored by mainstream feminism. Public female intellectuals still offer deterministic biological perspectives of what it means to be a woman, let alone a feminist. Naomi Wolf asserted in 2012, albeit to sizeable ridicule, that feminism somehow rested on "the happiness" of women's vaginas. Breastfeeding for extended periods without supplementing and home birth had become, in some quarters, the measure of success of women against a patriarchal medical establishment.

Alongside this essentialist tendency among feminists, there was also a more triumphal one that saw such signs as women's greater attendance at law schools as a crucial example of feminism's success. Indeed, women now dominate in many professional settings. In American universities in 2011, 57 percent of undergraduates were women. Single childless women under age thirty in metropolitan areas were earning more than single childless men in the same situation. But such statistics didn't tell the full story of feminism, which was interested not simply in school attendance but also in core identity shifts involving gender as well. The triumphal liberal feminism that celebrated the laudable but still somewhat narrow professional attainment of some groups of women—the large number working as accountants in America, for instance—did not tend to question gender categories themselves.

For Rey, Serano, and others like them, feminism had taken an unexpected twist and could be extended to include them as they profoundly challenged gender roles. Given that feminism has politicized what it means to have a female body, trans feminism actually does make sense as an extension of the feminist movement's corporeal concerns. But it can also be a challenge because the trans bodies in question aren't, to quote the well-known gender theorist Lady Gaga, "born this way."

Serano and company made swift headway in some areas. Organizations including the Third Wave Foundation claim that part of their agenda is to dispel "the myth that women's liberation and transgender liberation have opposing agendas." GenderPAC, which shut down in 2009, was a nonprofit that fought gender discrimination in public schools, serving both young women at risk and the "gender-nonconforming." Women's organizations, including the National Council for Research on Women (NCRW), have held events dedicated to the concept of gender and to transgender people in the corporate workplace. At one NCRW session, "Gender Identity in the Workplace," the moderator, Meryl Kaynard of JPMorgan, joked that a transwoman she knew had "broken the glass ceiling, just from a different direction." Today, biological women might offer insights that once would have belonged to gender outlaws. A young woman named Amanda Lineweber put it this way to me in an e-mail about gender activism on campus when she was a first-year student: "In past eras, what our parents call 'experimentation' has often been left behind as college students become older and join the larger world. In this era, however, the shift to thinking about gender and sexuality as fluid is happening in a more uniform and permanent way. We identify with different 'genders' at different intensities at different times in one's life. We reject the necessity of labels and definitions, and we refuse to define ourselves in order to make others comfortable. I can see these theories moving from a teenage phase to an accepted part of the human condition."

Thanks to concepts such as trans feminism, dozens of women's studies scholars started to rethink their nomenclature and curriculum. Many departments decided to relabel themselves as "gender studies" or "women's and gender studies" programs. While once "a white liberal version of feminism" dominated, scholar Judith Halberstam told me, where "men were clear oppressors of women and 'female' was a stable category, this is no longer true. In women's studies, people are bucking against these things. This is a huge shift. I mean, once, the accusation of being 'male identified' was a huge problem." Women's studies courses are "very pro-trans" now, she said. In the past, the same kinds of students who are transitioning or identifying as "gender-nonconforming" might have identified as gay, been confused and lost, or simply not questioned their gender identities at all. Now, a newly etched "trans identity" is visible and available to them. The philosopher Judith Butler revised her famous theory of "doing" gender to incorporate transgender people, positing that "undoing" gender is a crucial way of being male or female.

It's no surprise that some of the earliest instances of trans feminism happened at women's colleges. Activist Simon Aronoff, a thirty-six-year-old transman who lives in Chicago, began his transition in the 1990s, when he was still attending Smith. As a student, he worked to incorporate transgender issues into the school's Lesbian Bisexual Alliance, alongside a cadre of fellow students who were also coming out as men or as something in between. He continued to call himself a feminist. When Aronoff graduated from Smith College and entered the workforce, doing communications for gender rights and gay rights policy centers, he kept thinking that gender was being cordoned off as a transgender issue, separate from being gay. He felt his mission was to fight for "trans activism as feminism."

The problem is, Aronoff said in his soft southern accent, transpeople are often "filtered out" of the history of feminism. "I'd love to bridge gaps between feminist communities and queer communities," he said. "I know I have a female well of experiences that make me a stronger feminist." He said his own trans feminism came from having "a female history and a male social experience." He perceived gender politics differently because he had lived in two very different ways, he said.

For trans feminists, the concept that gender is a performance (an idea beloved in critical theory) is something they understand firsthand. For Serano, Rey, and others like them, this was the true radical new wave of feminism.

HIRSTORY

In the virtual, text-heavy world of the early Internet, many people found they could suddenly play with their gender—or anything else about themselves—online. Fifteen years after *Imagining Transgender* author and anthropologist David Valentine documented transpeople, he told me in an interview that he wondered whether younger gender nonconformers were more fluid in their gender orientation specifically *because* they were so Web-influenced—more protean, in part, due to the possibilities for flexible identities the Internet had popularized.

The Web plays a role in disseminating trans feminism as well as transgender liberation. On the Internet, gender-nonconforming people find community at younger ages but also learn about everything from the concept "trans feminism" to which doctors to see.

The True Selves site, for instance, bills itself as a "forum for Generation X & Y people who are transsexual and/or transgender, who are or want to be actively transitioning in some way." Individual bloggers arrayed across the gender continuum, such as Lisa Harney of Questioning Transphobia and those writing at the Transgender Boards, attract large groups of followers. On Tumblr, patients of Charles Garramone, a surgeon who performs mostly female-to-male (FTM) top surgeries, post sometimes graphic images of their postsurgical days: one person posted the caption "24 hours post-op/Drinking tea" to accompany an image of a transitioning person with a bandaged chest, while another post displayed the still-bright chest scars after top surgery and a third patient posted a video "reveal" of his chest being unbandaged. I can go to YouTube and watch a very compelling young transman named Joshua Bastian Cole talk about his life for twenty minutes; for Cole, the Web was his educator and survival kit when he was coming out. Younger transitioners can visit dating sites where they can search for people to meet while also discussing in detail their stage of transition, such as whether they want to be called *they* or *genderqueer* or *him* or *her*. Member profiles for a transpeople dating site that launched in 2012 detailed the variety of potential identities available in a new gender economy, from "boi" to "transfag."

As Thiessen put it, the people she met online were far more influential and helpful as she started to transition than the counselors who advised her in person on transitioning. She was going online constantly, reading forums and message boards written by people like her. "I learned most of what trans lives are like from the Internet," she said.

Thousands of parents of "gender-variant" kids—moms and dads who are raising boys who want to wear tunics and be called Anastasia or rearing girls who despise plastic dolls in baby carriages and are happier pushing around big plastic fire engines—are also meeting online. Gender Spectrum, which supports families who are raising gender-variant children, hosts an annual conference for parents and children where they can use pronouns and names as they please, and its website encourages the idea of living in the "in-between" spaces of gender. It and other groups across the country are another example of a counterpublic for which writing—books, lectures, manifestos, blogs, Tumblrs, tweets—is a tool for transformation and where transformed physical bodies can themselves be considered a kind of text. Such bodies have been, in a sense, written on, as if flesh itself were text to be edited and revised.

Rey's gender voyage, like those of so many of his generation, began when he typed the word *transgender* into Google. Throughout high school, he spent dozens of hours online, reading about transgender people. "The Internet is the best thing for transpeople," he announced as we sat in his dorm room and he thought back on that time. Living in the suburbs, he said, "online groups were an access point."

GENDER IMPERFECT

The gender rights movement has made strides and has become more visible and more mainstream in the last ten years. In 2008, 125 of the Fortune 500 companies included "gender identity" in their nondiscrimination policies. That number used to be zero. According to the HRC Corporate Equality Index, in 2013, 57 percent of the Fortune 500 companies will include "gender identity" in their nondiscrimination policies. That figure was at 3 percent in 2002. In 2009, an annual transgender career expo drew recruiters from companies such as Microsoft and Ernst & Young who met with women and men who have transitioned or are gender nonconforming. According to the LGBT advocacy group the Human Rights Campaign, the number and percentage of employers and colleges with transgender-inclusive health insurance, which includes hormones and sometimes surgeries, has risen within the past decade: in 2004, 1 percent of Fortune 100 companies had transgender-inclusive medical plans; in 2013, 25 percent of Fortune 500 companies would provide them. (However, the same report lists 42 percent of survey participants as offering transgender-inclusive benefits.) In the course of reporting this book, I met the first transgender representative at the venerable gay organization GLAAD and talked to a spokesperson for the first transgender lobbying group, the National Center for Transgender Equality (NCTE). But being able to organize transpeople, push online for more complex identities such as gender-fluid or trans feminist, get adequate insurance, or attend trans-specific job fairs doesn't always mean they live healthier lives or have more workplace protections, according to Dean Spade, a thirtysomething trans legal scholar and activist. He struck a cautionary note about transpeople's media moment; according to Spade, there are limits to all this new visibility. "There may be increasing visibility, but it is not getting safer for transpeople," he said, citing the large number of hate crimes and prejudice still directed at them.

Spade mostly lived in Los Angeles, in a sparsely furnished one-bedroom apartment and had a family of his own creation that includes his ex-boyfriend and a child, all of whom have adopted the last name Spade. When we met in a café, he was clad in a pressed button-down shirt. He had an intense speaking style, and his black eyebrows resembled arched commas when he argued a point. After growing up on welfare and spending years working with indigent transpeople as a lawyer, he was skeptical that seeing "more transpeople on TV, in movies, in law, on campuses" will change things for those with little access to colleges or well-meaning feminist organizations.

Spade was referring to all the examples in popular culture of various people bending, changing, or challenging gender: RuPaul's drag reality show; Thomas Beatie, a FTM transperson who became famous as "the pregnant man" and was interviewed on *The Oprah Winfrey Show*; Cher's daughter, Chastity Bono, talking on television about changing genders to become Chaz; the cable TV series *The L Word*, which ran on Showtime from 2004 to 2009 and featured a character who was a transman, a former lesbian trying to "pass" as a man. (A promiscuous, testosterone-addled fellow, he was frequently reviled by the show's fans.) On a more pleasant note, the *New York Times* has run many op-eds by a transgender writer,

Jennifer Finney Boylan, on gender issues. And of course, every movement needs a glossy magazine, and gender-nonconformers have *Candy*, with the requisite movie star—James Franco—on a cover. It could sometimes seem as if gender nonconformity had become the target of niche marketing and, like so many outsider and renegade cultures in this book, co-opted as a fashion or style used to make things like lipstick both cool and also somehow ironic.

Spade and other transpeople do worry that the community could go from being invisible to being vacuously, stereotypically visible—a "tranny media moment," one called it, defined by people like a "bizarre" pregnant man or Hollywood actors in drag. As of 2013, no matter how many trans blogs there are, the law has not caught up. NCTE fought for the passage of a federal antidiscrimination bill, the Employment Non-Discrimination Act (ENDA), which included protections for workers' gender identities. The bill was split into two, however, ENDA and GENDA (one without transgender rights, the second specifically geared toward transgender rights), before it even got to the floor of the House in 2007. The inclusive ENDA died in committee before reaching the floor. In 2013, advocates were still hoping to wend a new transgender-inclusive version through the House of Representatives and finally have it passed.

AN INSIDE JOB

After Rey started to transition in 2007, I didn't see him for a few months. The next time I did, the transformation from the person he was to the man he'd always wanted to be was startling. We met on a street corner near Columbia in Upper Manhattan on a cold but sunny day in January 2008. Rey was aglow, smiling and laughing. Accompanied by his girlfriend at the time, Melissa, he greeted me with a hug.

His bright demeanor, he said, was due to the changes he'd made. He had been going to the Callen-Lourde Community Health Center in Manhattan, a clinic for the LGBTQ population, for testosterone shots. (He had tried to get his parents to sign the consent form for transitioning when he was seventeen, but they refused, he said.) The shots he'd received every other week since October had lowered his voice a few octaves. Since we had last seen each other, Rey had gone through much of the rest of male puberty; he had increased bone mass and facial hair. He was also in the process of legally changing his given name to a male one, although he couldn't decide whether to go casual (Rey) or Old Testament (Asher). Rey wanted to blend in as a man and men don't usually have breasts, as he put it: he had had to bind his. In December 2007, Rey underwent top surgery, which he paid for out of pocket.

He co-founded GendeRevolution, the first transgender-specific club that Columbia University had ever had, one of the first trans advocacy groups at an Ivy League school. To cap it off, he was bar mitzvahed in January. As a girl, he had had his bat mitzvah at age thirteen, but, as Rey put it, he didn't feel "connected to the experience." His parents did not attend his bar mitzvah, he said, because he did it in Israel. But he took the rite of passage to heart. Now, at eighteen, he was a man not only in his own eyes but also in the eyes of his faith.

"Before I was on hormones, people would get confused when I spoke to them over the phone and they didn't know me. They thought I was male, and then they'd start asking questions about how old I was," Rey recalled. "I didn't want to stay a prepubescent boy."

Even so, Rey continued to lead the life of a college student: going to clubs, focusing on keeping up his grades. He got more involved with campus gender awareness. At Columbia University's Office of Multicultural Affairs, he organized a series of trans awareness events on campus and was paid by the college to do so. When we met in late January, he had two chores on his list: booking a transmale photographer as a speaker and creating signage for gender-neutral bathrooms. He was busy sketching possible new symbols. In one sketch, he turned the familiar female stick figure into a rocket ship, making her legs into a flame. He created a few variations of the sign with a ballpoint pen. Then he drew a confused-looking person standing in front of both a male and a female bathroom, not knowing which one to pick. Next, he tried a single circle with the male and female symbols attached to it.

Melissa had previously defined herself as a lesbian. Rey's transition "made sense" to her, she said. Her sangfroid felt generational: these two saw gender not as a rigid inevitability but as a fluid aspect of existence, susceptible to personal choice. Like some of their peers, Rey and his friends want to be—and sometimes imagine they already are—part of the first generation to transcend gender altogether. "I think gender is a spectrum," Rey said to me.

Transitioning was, in its way, a profoundly American idea. It rested on a concept of a new kind of self in which everyone should be able to pursue and achieve happiness, to transform old ways into something radically different. They fit into the American notion of self-making and self-reinvention but turned those notions in a fresh direction. Transitioning from one gender to another medically is a decades-old phenomenon, and living in ambiguous spaces between genders was, in fact, a well-documented ancient practice. But Rey and the others I spoke to were now transitioning not only into a new gender identity but also into a new kind of feminism.

I next saw Rey six months after our January meeting. His transformation was complete. But he was still a twenty-year-old, experiencing all sorts of other transitions typical of that age. He could be a giddy teenager, smoking and showing up late for an appointment. Less frequently he was pensive and moody, especially when he found himself considering the vexing issues faced by transgender people about their place and acceptance in society.

He had broken up with Melissa and now defined himself even more clearly as an activist. I met him with his friend Julia, a sylph-like young woman who had an emphatic speaking style and a Jean Seberg haircut. She was very eager to tell me how Rey had changed the way she saw her own biologically female identity and in the process had influenced other "gender-normal" students in the college. That day, Rey had his hair up in short black dreads wrapped in a bandanna. He looked like a skater boy. His T-shirt bore the legend "Tranny."

Rey had been writing a lot. A few weeks after that meeting, he sent me some of his writings, including links to his "trans group on Facebook called 'the trans community,'" adding, "This group is for everyone!!! Part of transitioning through anything is part of realizing that you don't have to identify with what people tell you that you are supposed to be." In an essay titled "Gender Is a Circle," he was more emotionally direct:

> I have felt the pressure of the gender binary from both sides. When I was a kid, my mother made me wear dresses. . . . My dad tells me I look like Sinéad O'Connor and that I should let my hair grow out. I was never trying

to be a man. I was never trying to be a woman. I was always and I am still just being myself. I was born into a female body, but my mind was more complex. The choices
I was given in this world, unfortunately, were to either
transition with medical intervention or just keep having
to explain that my gender doesn't match my physical sex.

Rey and others on similar quests had taken something as fundamental as gender and questioned it loudly and publicly. Their lives
and deeds showed that complicating gender could be a big threat
to the order of things but also could lead, in small ways, to change.

"Some transmen want to be accepted as born men," said Rey.
"I want to be accepted as a transman. My brain is not gendered.
There's this crazy gender binary that's built into all of life, that
there are just two genders that are acceptable. I don't want to
have to fit into that."

Like so many Americans, transpeople and trans feminists were
also captives of what some academics call postcapitalism. They
were attempting to get back to something rooted in personal experience, doing their best to reject prefabricated tastes and preset
identities and arriving at surprising new combinations. It was often an uphill battle, and not simply due to negative stereotypes.

In 2011, Barnard College offered a trial of its first gender-
neutral housing, partially thanks to Rey's activism three years
earlier. It was a small step for transpeople and gender-fluid people
that indicated a larger shift.

When I checked in on Rey a few years later, in 2012 and
then in 2013, he had graduated from Columbia University. Like
many other people of his generation, he had a hipster five o'clock
shadow, was unemployed, and had moved back home with his

parents, to a suburb of New York City, while he looked for a job. "It's lame: my life is on hold till I get one," he said.

Even though his future employment remained a question mark, Rey's thinking and internal life had clarified since he graduated. He felt that what he called "trans awareness" also had "exploded even since I started transitioning—I haven't had to explain being trans to anyone in a really long time." For his parents, his trans identity was now a "nonissue," he said. "They joke about it. My dad took me to an endocrinologist so I could move on to [testosterone] gel rather than injections. My mother even wrote an essay about transpeople in the workplace."

He was trying, he said, to become more self-sufficient and get his own apartment. He was taking classes in counseling with the aim of being a "peer specialist." "I wasn't prepared for the competitive job market and wasn't sure what to do with myself" after graduating, he said. "I had to shift my goals from art and music to a more consistent and realistic way of making money."

In the meantime, Rey had met "tons" of transpeople living in the city, and in Westchester he met older gender-nonconforming people who had not yet transitioned. He had reached the point where he felt comfortable issuing advice to others: "One transperson in his forties said he didn't want to transition and 'feel like a freak,' and I told him that a lot of transpeople nowadays have bodies that are halfway male, halfway female, and they are not categorized. If you feel comfortable with the way your body is, another person will as well. It's an inside job to feel comfortable."

Rey was constantly surprised by how much had changed in genderqueer culture, even in the nearly six years since I had first met him as a freshman, and certainly from the moment when he first had an inkling he was trans back in high school. The language around the movement has shifted, he said. And then there was "YouTube and blogs" and a whole new kind of gender fluidity, as he put it.

"People nowadays aren't just reproducing the biological gender binary when they transition," Rey continued. "For instance, my friends who are women don't think of me as a regular man, and that's great—they think I am more aware, more sensitive, more able to identify" with women.

"When I am with groups that are all men, I think about trans feminism," he said. "The guys would say the kind of sexist things young guys sometimes say, and it makes me really uncomfortable. I usually say something. Trans feminism is still just as important to me as it ever was."

Rey hoped that transpeople and their thinking about gender-as-spectrum would move the mainstream. With nearly everything he said, Rey, like other "outsiders" I met, was a cultural entrepreneur of a sort, selling an idea of transformation to a broader public as well as consuming it himself. He and his peers were creating the ideas they needed to nourish their sense of self. They were propelled by the broad and nearly sacrosanct American belief that the point of life was happiness, and they felt they could achieve that happiness if they could just alter the gender norms they were born into.

They were innovating their own identities but also trying to alter feminism itself. Transcending and remixing sex stereotypes, they believed, was a necessary next stage for the development of both men and women. In order to obtain greater equality for all, they thought, we must look again at how gender biases and clichés limit all of us.

3

BEYOND NORMAL

"I don't care about being seen as weird," a young woman named Katie told me after she had picked me up at the train station and was driving me to her apartment nearby. She was clad in a bright blue fake-fur jacket a few shades brighter than Cookie Monster, truck-yellow clogs, and oversize sunglasses with blingy fake crystals running up the sides. Her clothes were so bright they almost made the record cold day in Baltimore a little warmer. The streets were piled high with ice and sleet, and to get to the house where she then lived by herself, you had to slush through a wall of snow.

Inside, her place was also brightly decorated with an acid-green chair and a grape-purple couch. In the corner were her gargantuan furry slippers, also rainbow-colored. Her books were organized by size and by color: purple, indigo, and blue books on the left, yellow and green in the middle, red on the right. Her walk-in closet, painted with all the Skittles colors, looked like a psychedelic vintage store in Haight-Ashbury. She showed me her miniature elephant collection: hundreds of them, plastic and ceramic. She took out a piece of blue felt dabbed in jasmine perfume. Whenever ordinary smells, like smoke or fish, over-whelmed her, she sniffed the blue fabric. She told me about her life in granular detail: each morning she woke up, put on makeup and an outfit, and ate vanilla almond cereal with skim milk. And from time to time, she exclaimed out loud things other people don't tend to say, like that her earring just fell down her bra.

Katie, who is twenty-nine and who asked me to refer to her only by her first name, is part of a growing outsider community that has used the Web to make its presence known to—and to help move—the mainstream. She's autistic and part of a new, mostly Web-based movement often referred to as "neurodiversity" or "autistic rights." Her outsider microcosm strives to redefine how America thinks not just about autism but also about normality itself. Her movement takes aim at a central tenet of ordinary American society: it questions whether there really is, or should be, a normal way for all of us to emote, process experience and information, and interact with others.

Katie and the rest of the neurodiverse crowd have a neurologically based disability. Some might classify Katie as having either Asperger's syndrome or "high-functioning" autism, although she disputes the very existence of Asperger's as a separate condition and prefers to call herself autistic. Many in the American Psychiatric Association agree with her. A proposed (and controversial) change to the fifth edition of the *DSM*, due out in 2013, would combine Asperger's and autism into a single diagnosis: autism spectrum disorder.

"I don't 'have autism'—I'm autistic. In the same way you wouldn't say you 'have femaleness,' you'd say you are a woman," Katie explained.

Katie and others like her believe, quite reasonably, that they know their own minds best. But they also think they know "neurotypicals"—ordinary people—better than neurotypicals know themselves. (When the neurodiverse use the term *neurotypical*, they mean people whose minds are wired to operate more conventionally than those of Katie and her ilk.) Some believe the neurotypicals are more neurodiverse or more autistic than they admit to being. Their central claim is that "normal" is just an arbitrary cutoff point on the spectrum. Autistic activists like to talk about what they call "the broader phenotype," by which they mean people who have a few autistic traits but not enough to be diagnosed with Asperger's syndrome. Like the transpeople and the Mad Pride contingent, the neurodiverse want the neurotypical to acknowledge the oddities and outlying traits in all of us and recognize the useful qualities of our weirdness—and, by extension, the value of their more obvious weirdness. As was true of many of the outsiders I met, their movement existed in a state of tension: were they happily different from normal people or were they superior to the mainstream?

We all experience many states that we share with the neurodiverse. For instance, like Katie, many neurotypicals frequently have highly overwhelming sensory experiences that they sometimes fear. Like Katie, many of us don't always want to make eye contact, especially with authority figures. The brains of people on the autism spectrum can be wired to respond strongly to colors and surfaces, but neurotypicals, too, can have a strong reaction to brightly colored, textured clothing. Autistic people are likely to want to avoid bright, loud places such as beaches or public squares; "normal" people often share such sensitivities. Similarly, many neurotypicals also memorize every possible detail about irrelevant things or linger in front of laptop computer screens, the light reflecting in their eyes, rather than chat with others face-to-face. Facebook and other social networking sites are supposedly full of neurotypicals who connect to others in more direct ways than Katie and her cohort on the extreme end of the neurodiversity spectrum. But autism activists see social media as part of "autism culture": their friendships are more likely to develop in online social networks, due to the relative emotional safety they find in the virtual. After all, in-person encounters can induce emotional overload or moments of shocking spontaneity for autistic people.

My encounters with neurodiverse people tended to begin with some of that overload. They told me long, circumlocutory stories. They loved lists. They delighted in words unto themselves. They displayed a rapt interest in small units of time; obsessive detailing of information and trivia (was the ham sandwich thrown at their fellow activists during a rally actually a burrito?); fear of unearned closeness (all that eye contact!); and a marked, yet usually self-obstructed, desire for intimate attachment. Some of them told me about their experiences at an Autism Pride celebration, a relatively new event held every June 18. They might wear T-shirts with quasi-hilarious, pro-"neuro" slogans such as "Eye Contact Is Overrated," "I Don't Do Small Talk," or "Autistic Genius." There was one narrative, though, that every one of them touched on at some point: the story of the unexpected power of autistic culture.

"If I may stereotype you: You neurotypicals like socializing late at night, loud places, frequent and varied greetings, and social customs," Katie said. She extended her fingers: her fingernails were painted an unearthly pale green, like the inside of a mother-of-pearl ashtray. Why is almost every restaurant so loud? she wondered. Why do neurotypicals act as if they like pulsing techno or screechy music? After all, how could they?

Katie and neurodiverse bloggers I met or read were on quests for their authentic selves—quests often stymied in an America that requires constant work and often a willingness to adapt one's "real self" in order to survive economically. The market and other economic forces shape so much of who we are, after all, as does a lockstep sort of socialization. But within the marketplace of ideas and social attitudes, the neurodiverse cannot entirely escape capitalism, of course. They, too, have something to sell, something to market, such as the concepts "neurodiversity" and autism culture. They are entrepreneurs of self: self-starters, self-identifiers. They are creating new desires and needs and selling the means to fulfill them. Their "profit" will be acceptance on a personal level and also transforming the way everyone—autistic people as well as "normal" people, including policy makers—think about autism.

Many among the neurodiverse believe that autism plays a critical role in such fields as engineering, advanced mathematics, and geek culture. Studies have repeatedly shown that minds made for mechanical engineering or computer technology often share many traits with those on the spectrum. Simon Baron-Cohen, one of the leading researchers on autism and director of the Autism Research Centre at Cambridge University (he also happens to be the cousin of comedian Sacha Baron Cohen), has found that 12 percent of the grandfathers and fathers of autistic people worked in engineering fields. In the nonautistic population, only 5 percent had engineers for dads and granddads. And it may also work the other way: some scholars believe the same genetics that produce autism are more likely to produce mathematical and computer science skills than more typical genetics.

These are the sorts of things the neurodiverse want you to know about.

In other words, what many neurotypicals see as a disability, the neurodiverse see as the crux of American culture. Some of them believe that this is nothing less than the age of autism. For them, everything from peer-to-peer downloads to video games to social networking reflects the rise of an autistic sensibility. Anything that thrives on the sort of systematic, superrational thought that characterizes autism or Asperger's—computer programming or even the obsessive collecting done by collage artists—fits into the autism culture narrative. The neurodiverse believe autism is not simply a disease to be cured but something between a disability and a different way of seeing the world. They are trying to wrest autism out of a professional medical context and bring it into a personal, cultural one. Some make a distinction between high-functioning autistics and those who can't communicate at all or manage minimal care of themselves. (A number of activists, including Katie, dislike this distinction; indeed, she claims this category "does not exist," as it has no "agreed-upon meaning" and is "considered offensive by many," including her.) Numbers are hard to come by, but it's estimated that 70 percent of autistic children are considered high-functioning, albeit with communication and social challenges. Another estimate had a third of autistic people as functioning relatively easily and a third to be very disabled, with one-third in between. Within the neurodiverse community, there are people who define themselves as autistic and those who would rather see themselves as Asperger's syndrome folk or Aspies: the talented third, if you will, of autistic people. And they are using the Web to disseminate their rallying word, *neurodiversity*.

Katie is one of the most engaging neurodiversity activists I've met. I could see how having a "different kind of wiring" could be worth celebrating, how being neurodiverse could open a person up to unlikely connections between things, allowing the mind to see the number 1 as white and 2 as green. Such visual connections made sense for Katie, who has since graduated from Maryland Institute College of Art. "Being autistic has affected my vision of the world, which has affected my art," she told me. "I notice different things than other people do about color, shape, and pattern."

When Katie was a child growing up in Florida and California, her parents dismissed her obsessive behavior as the quirks of a young artist. And to some extent they were. She could spend an entire day sketching or copying pictures out of books. "I'd throw a fit if I couldn't draw something right," Katie recalled. But as she grew older, she became more withdrawn.

In high school, Katie saw a psychologist for anxiety and depression. Another professional diagnosed her as having obsessive-compulsive disorder, but when she saw an OCD specialist, she was "undiagnosed," as she put it. None of their assessments, however, seemed to capture Katie's mind.

"We'd never even heard of Asperger's," explained Katie's father, a retired engineer. When she enrolled in the College of Art, where she earned both a bachelor's degree and an MFA, Katie began researching her symptoms online and concluded that she might have autism. At first her friends and parents thought she was wrong to believe she had autism; she was just shy or maybe a little too artsy for this world, they argued. While it was true she was both shy and artsy, there was more to her condition, more to her state of mind. Katie can't handle intense stimulation. If she hears a loud noise, she has to cover her ears because it's so painful, she said. She gets overstimulated by spicy or bright foods, so she eats only chicken fingers and pasta and avoids most vegetables. And when her intense sensitivities were activated, Katie melted down, cried, threw up, or just stood frozen in place. Sometimes she flapped her hands, a self-soothing behavior common among autistic people. Finally, in college, she presented her findings to a neuropsychologist, who confirmed her suspicions. "It was definitely a relief to find out what was really going on," said Katie.

Katie's diagnosis immediately brought her into the online autism community, which in turn brought her to autistic gatherings such as Autreat, where participants are encouraged to wear badges to indicate whether they want friends or strangers to come up and talk to them or not. The people at Autreat also flap their hands instead of clapping after each speaker, since the noise of applause can disturb some autistic people. In her daily life, Katie sometimes wears Autism Pride T-shirts with slogans such as "Celebrate Neurodiversity" and "I Only Look Neurotypical." She told everyone at her art school that she is autistic. She is online constantly, doing battle with people who, she said, deny she's really autistic: parents of autistic children "hating on her," trolls who comment that she is "not really autistic because you can read."

"We don't all wear diapers and butt our heads!" Katie said. She nonetheless refused to concede that there are substantial differences between "high-functioning" autistic people such as her and "low-functioning" autistic people. It's not that she doesn't want the significant proportion of autistic people who also have low IQs to get the help they need. (According to the National Institute on Deafness and Other Communication Disorders, experts estimate that 25 percent of children with autism are too verbally impaired to develop spoken language skills.) But it's clear that Katie's intense desire to define autism as a beneficial, valuable, and productive identity leads her to deemphasize the dark side. Also, like some of the neurodiverse, she shudders at the idea that money is being poured into the search for a cure for autism instead of being directed toward services for autistic people. She objects to what she sees as deleterious labels used to describe autism. She claims she doesn't see autism as an impediment—it doesn't make her lesser, only different.

When Katie says the Web has changed her life, she doesn't mean the Web of e-commerce but rather an incarnation of cyberspace, the world of innovations that gives individuals tools to do things once possible only for powerful companies and institutions. The Web gave a previously silent population a chance to influence the mainstream.

Of course, living comfortably as an autistic person day to day can be hard. Katie's life isn't easy, especially because being autistic makes complicated social situations confusing. When she goes to a party with mostly neurotypicals, she will stand still, often unable to meet or speak to anyone, unnerved by the noise in the room, and gets so overstimulated she will quickly retreat home. She can't read facial expressions easily. When I mentioned shortly after I met her in 2010 that one of her art school friends, a woman who had braided Katie's hair like Princess Leia's earlier in the day and applied her makeup, had "a kind face," Katie looked befuddled.

"What confuses me is when people mask their true feelings, such as act kind or polite but are actually annoyed, or more subtle things like that," she explained a few years later. "Or sometimes if someone I don't know very well jokes with a straight face, I might not know they are joking." She worried about romance being difficult, even though she's a glowing blonde with a lovely smile and even, elegant features. It was just that when she met a man, she couldn't tell whether he was interested in her or not.

The CDC estimates that one in eighty-eight American children is on the autistic spectrum, and of those, roughly 80 percent are boys. Some even have claimed that we are in the midst of an "autism epidemic"—a controversial notion, since the rise in documented cases may be a reflection of a change in diagnosis patterns. Because the disorder is so commonly associated with boys, women are notoriously underdiagnosed. "Girls are better at overcompensating for their autism, perhaps because they usually have better communication skills or because the drive for social conformity is more pronounced for them," explained Baron-Cohen in an e-mail interview. It's easier to discern a problem in a boy who obsessively memorizes baseball stats going back fifty years, but a girl whose autism is expressed by meticulously drawing pictures or who has difficulty making eye contact is a less obvious candidate. "Professionals are worse at detecting autism in females," he concluded.

Katie can't always "pass" in a world with loud noises. When she was still in art school, we went to a pizza place near the school for dinner, and she immediately grew uncomfortable: the song "My Funny Valentine" was playing loudly in the background, a video game was bleeping, and there were conversations at tables all around us. At moments like this, she often would put on her big green Day-Glo headphones, the same kind construction workers use to protect their ears from the sound of drilling. When a conversation or the imperative to try to make eye contact got to be too much for her, she squeezed a soft plastic dinosaur toy; she did this off and on as we talked.

She also socialized less frequently than many people. But when I celebrated her twenty-sixth birthday with her, it was a joint party for her and two of her fellow students, an art school gathering. Katie's wild fashion sense blended right in with that of the other partygoers. One had arrived at the party clad as a sexy mermaid. A red-haired male art student who could be considered a classic art school type, painting images based on his teenage depression, talked to Katie in a corner. The group sat around listening to music, drinking wine, and eating carrot cake. Occasionally Katie neared the edge of overstimulation: when a few balloons accidentally popped, she looked terrified. But a beat later, she was laughing and talking again.

During that visit, we went to her studio at school. She showed me her paintings of infants: lovely, eerie pictures of an isolated, blankly staring child holding a lollipop. Katie's babies and children appear simultaneously oddly old and oddly young. The paintings get at what she and other autistic people know all too well: what it is like to be a sage adult in some ways and a defenseless person in others, *at the same time*. As Katie put it, her work is informed by the sense that an "autistic person is on the same level as her peers and in others they are years behind." Her excellent draftsmanship and awry perspective were part of why she received prizes and has already had gallery shows. And Katie's photorealist draftsmanship—her ability to paint with an almost photographic quality—may be related to being autistic. Though scientists and doctors can't always explain it, many with the condition have incredible mathematical, musical, or artistic talents. Some experts speculate it may have something to do with the obsessive repetitive behaviors that children with autism develop—they tend to "practice" their craft more intensely and with greater focus than other children. "I owe my painting to a lifetime of focus," explained Katie. "I had a bit of natural ability but mostly an intense interest and drive. I wasn't drawing amazing things when I was a little kid. But I drew a lot, a lot, a lot. I kept at it more than most."

ON A DIFFERENT PLANET

The autism site Wrong Planet, which evaluates media and cultural portrayals of autism, has tens of thousands of members, hosts millions of posts, and is a hub for people across the autism spectrum. Alex Plank, Wrong Planet's founder, created the site in college; he told me its name derives from his feeling that he and others like him are not themselves "wrong" or "off," but simply have landed on an unyielding and rather disturbing place—planet Earth. On Wrong Planet, he said, many with autism who can't literally vocalize speech but can write get to "speak" through their written Internet posts.

"If all people communicated entirely on the Internet, we autistic people wouldn't have a problem," Plank said. "The way that we are forced to interact—the way *people* are forced to interact—is not even natural," he continued during an amiable conversation that nevertheless reflected some of his inherent beliefs that talking is unnatural; at one point, he exchanged sharp words with his friend and interrupted our chat to ask many, many questions of a café's waitress about what was in a certain salad. In a later telephone conversation, he told me, "It's a by-product of certain social norms, of all these manners—manners that differ from place to place."

Thousands of other bloggers on the autism spectrum have joined online discussions of autism, and some of them have become intensely popular, attracting large followings. Neurodiversity advocate Amanda Baggs blogs at Ballastexistenz and has appeared on television, including CNN. There's the popular autism news and science blog Left Brain Right Brain. There are also autism blogs by people such as Orac, a self-proclaimed "surgeon/scientist" who uses his blog to attack persistent (despite being repeatedly debunked) claims that vaccines cause autism.

Such neurodiverse online communities now act as shadow social services. On the Web, Katie and people like her may have to wade through a lot of bad science about causes of autism, but they also find useful checklists of traits and make contact with nearby people like them whom they can then meet.

They know they have their work cut out for them, and some strive to organize politically online. In 2007, Wrong Planet's Plank and Ari Ne'eman, founder of the Autistic Self Advocacy Network (ASAN), organized opposition to an advertising campaign by New York University's Child Study Center that portrayed autism as one of many psychiatric and neurological disorders that hold twelve million children "hostage." Plank and Ne'eman believed the ads falsely represented autism as a purely monstrous thing. They argue that science—and society at large—should see the autistic's differences in neurological development and functioning as singular and valuable, striving to understand those differences rather than labeling them as damaged or imprisoning. "Stimming" (behaviors such as flapping hands) and avoiding eye contact are symptoms of autism that some neurodiverse say don't need to be cured. Some neurodiverse advocates call those who seek to cure autism "cure-bes."

If the autism of these people were eliminated, they wouldn't exist as distinct individuals, the advocates say. After they finished rallying and writing indignant Web posts, they told me that ad campaigns such as the NYU Child Study Center's raised bigotry rather than awareness. Ultimately, their grassroots campaign got the advertising pulled.

Ne'eman, a twenty-five-year-old autism rights advocate who founded ASAN right after high school, became the first autistic adult appointed to President Barack Obama's National Council on Disability in 2010. His group has become a highly visible and engaged advocacy organization, describing itself as "advancing self-advocacy, self-determination, self-awareness, and independent living throughout all aspects of society." But opposition to these last two goals in particular—which were constant refrains of the neurodiverse advocates I spoke to—were a crucial element in slowing down Ne'eman's nomination to the council. Ne'eman's critics said his group's aims were unrealistic for many autistic people and that Ne'eman himself represented only the so-called talented third on the autism spectrum—those who have good communication skills and who are already autonomous. (Such critics tended to ignore the fact that Ne'eman attended special schools for his disability for much of his academic life.) "He doesn't seem to represent, understand or have great sympathy for all the people who are truly, deeply affected in a way that he isn't," Jonathan Shestack, co-founder of the advocacy group Cure Autism Now, told the *New York Times*.

Roy Richard Grinker is an anthropologist of autism at George Washington University and the author of a book on autism called *Unstrange Minds*. He's also the father of Isabel, a twenty-one-year-old woman with autism. He thought of the neurodiverse as a step forward for autism. "The people who are opposing Ari Ne'eman and people like him are people who want him—and autism—to be seen as a living hell," said Grinker, his tone scathing. "It's like those memoirs by autistic parents who all say something like 'My child's soul was taken; I want to bring him out.' Ari Ne'eman and the neurodiverse are contesting the medical model and contesting that autism is a homogenous entity. One of the key differences is that the medical model says that there is something wrong with that person, while the neurodiverse and people like them argue that it is a disability and there is something wrong with the environment."

Grinker had his own complex feelings about the neurodiverse community's refusal of pathological labels and the tendency to portray all such labels as stigmatizing. Labels and certified medical diagnoses are necessary for parents to get their children school accommodations, treatment, or help. But as the father of Isabel, who was aided by her diagnosis of autism, he believed that even though his daughter didn't know the term *neurodiversity*, helping people understand autism as an enormous spectrum can only benefit her.

"The neurodiverse are saying, 'If you want to cure us, you want to eradicate us; if you eliminated the biopathways that lead to neurodiversity, you would eliminate the things that make humans different; if you wipe out the genes implicated in autism, would that destroy human creativity, as autistic traits don't just exist in autistic people?'" explained Grinker.

He expressed anger at other autism activists who make claims about autism's causes that are absolutely contradicted by science: that childhood vaccinations cause the diseases and that the use of mercury in kids' shots has led to an autism epidemic. (The "vaccines cause autism" community is composed of people who are outsiders and renegades in their own, albeit quite effective, way. They have successfully used the Web as well, much as the neurodiverse have, and have been brilliant in publicizing their cause.)

In sharp contrast, Grinker pointed out the value and the reach of neurodiversity in the life of his daughter Isabel. She worked at a zoo, minding groups of small children as they toured the facilities. This played to her strengths: his daughter was adept at ensuring that any set of anything—children, cookies, personal belongings—stayed whole and that no piece went missing. This was one attribute of her being a person with autism. Grinker wondered whether it would have been possible for her to get that job before neurodiversity advocacy and other channels of autism pride had endorsed the autistic mind.

"People are appreciating what skills she has not despite her having autism but as part of who she is," said Grinker. The neurodiverse helped show how she could create a workable, salable identity even without her being aware of the movement. The catch is that many autistic people are gleefully abnormal people in a world thought to value normality. They crash up against a country hell-bent on cheery, polished self-promotion. By rejecting conventional social behaviors and smooth, businesslike interactions, they are rejecting the ethos of self-help and the ethos of public relations. They are creating a culture at odds with so much America stands for, yet one that is strangely attractive to some outside the movement and part of a new way that "normals" may see—and want to see—themselves.

When the psychiatrist Leo Kanner wrote the earliest psychiatric case studies of autism, he described an autistic child as one who moved "like a stranger" among other people and skittered when confronted with face-to-face contact. Everyday social transactions were difficult for children with autism, he wrote, as was conceiving of language as a way of receiving and giving out meaningful information.

Decades later, in the 1960s and 1970s, the disability rights movement took off, with its catchphrase "Nothing about us without us." By that, disability rights activists meant "Let our sense of ourselves be part of any picture of us; put us in medical meetings or policy discussions where the professionals discuss our fate." These ideas were necessary precursors of the thinking behind neurodiversity.

As scholar Nancy Bagatell wrote in her 2010 essay "From Cure to Community: Transforming Notions of Autism," autistic people started applying an awareness of the goals and approaches of the disability-rights movement to their own cause in the 1990s. It was then that adults with autism first looked to autism organizations. At that time, most of those organizations were headed by parents of kids with autism or were meant for neuroscientists and doctors studying and treating autism.

The parent-run groups didn't satisfy the needs of a nascent movement of autistic adults, however. In the early 1990s, a group of them started Autism Network International, likely the first organization created by and for autistic people. Hundreds of groups have started since then, including ASAN. In 1993, some of the precepts behind these groups were laid out in the essay "Don't Mourn for Us" by Jim Sinclair, a person with autism, published in the newsletter of Autism Network International. The word *neurodiversity* was coined a few years later, in 1999, by an Australian woman named Judy Singer, whose child had Asperger's syndrome and who also saw herself as having some of the syndrome's traits. She said she saw the word as celebrating being on the autism spectrum.

The neurodiverse used the Web both to communicate and to create their identities. As Harvey Blume wrote, for autistic people Internet communication is like another nonauditory form of connection: Braille. "In cyberspace," Blume wrote in the *New York Times* in 1997, "many of the nation's autistics are doing the very thing the syndrome supposedly deters them from doing—communicating."

While the neurotypical can be confused emotionally by online chats and posts—the lack of tone of voice and facial cues sometimes confound people's understanding of e-mails, for instance—that very lack of tone online is a plus for a person with autism. Online communication also removes distracting elements, such as facial expressions, that autistic people tend not to understand well anyway. For autistic people, who can seem particularly inept at direct communication, the Web has freed them from such limitations.

The first decade of the 2000s has brought the dawn of the "autistic celebrity," showing how skillful the neurodiversity outsiders have been at innovating identity for the mainstream. One example is Bram Cohen, the founder of BitTorrent (a wildly successful tech company that helps millions of people freely, and sometimes illegally, exchange giant stores of digital information), who has repeatedly said in interviews that he has Asperger's syndrome. Cohen defined himself as being on the autism spectrum and the neurodiverse community has proudly claimed him, casting him as a sterling example of what's possible when a neurodiverse mind is set free to create and to build. Look what can happen, they say, when people stop trying to fund a cure for autism and simply celebrate it.

Yet while Cohen may have great understanding of patterns and computers, he does less well with ordinary interactions. He will not shake hands or tolerate small talk; he grew up with no friends but could program computers in three languages from an early age. In his late twenties, he spent nine months writing a peer-to-peer file-sharing protocol that helped change how people accessed and watched movies, television shows, and videos. For people like him, being basically friendless while running a company that relied on connecting people online wasn't novel—rather, it was a prime indicator of how autism culture had moved the mainstream by normalizing such online interactions. These achievements were emblematic of a clever, single-minded, technological, and transgressive sensibility at work. Cohen's celebrity as an out neurodiverse person was appealing to autism activists and journalists alike, showing that a person could make millions of dollars but have trouble making friends—that he could be both disabled and more skilled than his peers. This was part of a general tendency I noticed: some of the neurodiverse autistic people I spoke to and read held up autism as if it were a secret talisman.

To some, autism is an undesirable glitch in the complicated wiring of the brain, while the neurodiverse may see autism as part of a spectrum of all people's "different" brains. Others may speculate that some of history's most successful and creative people had autism; Albert Einstein is often mentioned, but no such diagnosis has been confirmed. A focused intelligence as well as a stilted social demeanor, mechanical abilities, uncanny memory: these can be read as autistic traits but also as the keys to success of some of the leading lights in Silicon Valley. (Notably, Silicon Valley has the country's highest rates of autism in children.)

For those who see the traits of autism in a positive light, the difference of minds should be respected, not isolated and "treated." Autistic people should receive services or support. (These are often collectively referred to with the term *treatment*, Katie pointed out, "but many of us may take issue with the word *treatment*, because it implies disease, and it is true that many of the 'treatments' for autism are quite abusive.")

On Wrong Planet, Alex Plank interviewed economist Tyler Cowen, who argued that there are "cognitive advantages held by a lot of autistics." The Web gives us "small bits, like a tweet or a blog post," Cowen told Plank, adding, "Living in a world where we manipulate small bits effectively" means "we are using information technology to mirror or mimic capabilities of autistics without usually people knowing it." Plank summed it up this way: the "autistic mode of thought can be more beneficial in certain situations."

Another famous person—perhaps *the* most famous person—with autism is Temple Grandin, a renowned designer of cattle-handling systems, an influential theorist of the animal mind and humane treatment of animals, and a bestselling author. "The same traits that make someone like Temple Grandin autistic also make her successful in vet science, that she is kind and helpful to animals," said Grinker. And more so-called normal people may have traits in common with Grandin than they might realize, he added. "Perhaps a person with six pet cats, who is incredible with them, may be a soft phenotype or a subclinical example of a person with autism."

The famed neurologist and writer Oliver Sacks profiled

Grandin in his book *An Anthropologist on Mars*, crediting her with breaking boundaries by exploring her condition. She had developed animal-sensitive ways to transport and even to kill livestock that changed the way the cattle and food industries functioned, giving them new dimensions of empathy. She famously said that she could do so because she was autistic and thus could think the way animals think. Grandin claims she does not "think in language," and neither do animals, thinking instead in pictures. Her success and influence are held up by the neurodiverse community as yet more evidence that autism is not a diminishment of capacity but a useful variation of it: autistic people have a primarily visual intelligence, and sometimes that "disability" can transform whole industries.

When I spoke to Grandin, she was dressed, as is her wont, "eccentrically," in a uniform of Western shirt, Western tie, and blue jeans. She was proud of her oddities and explained to me that, because she was brought up in the 1950s, she said "please" and "thank you" and tried not to be rude. "Good manners helped me adjust to the world," she told me. She mentioned that her fame as a figure of autistic pride was apexing with a biographical HBO film, *Temple Grandin*, which aired in 2010. Featuring the star Claire Danes as Grandin, it went on to win five Emmy Awards.

Grandin was quite matter-of-fact about the role autistic characteristics have played among highly functioning people. "I've met many people in technical fields—professors I had in college, other supertalented people—who cannot dress themselves," she said. "I work in a technical field, and I see Asperger's people functioning really well, fixing copying machines or working as newspaper reporters.

"If you get rid of autism genetics," Grandin went on, there

would be "no computer, no phone, and no Internet." Some of this talk was swagger, of course. But she had scientifically demonstrated reasons to be macho about autism culture. Some studies seem to suggest that genes that give rise to engineering and computing talent could also produce autism when they function in the "wrong" combination. But this is just one of many hypotheses; other potential causes include environmental factors, compromised maternal immunity, and even older fathers.

People such as Grandin and Cohen are folk heroes to the neurodiverse. And many of them would say their success on the Internet results in part from the advantages conferred by their autistic traits.

There are those who argue against neurodiversity, however. Matthew Belmonte, an assistant professor in the Department of Human Development at Cornell University, studies autism; he worries that neurodiversity, and its quest for self-actualization and self-assertion, could stymie the search for a cure. Many parents of autistic children find neurodiversity activist groups particularly enraging. They often feel overwhelmed by the problems presented by their children's condition, and neurodiversity seems to them a dangerous distraction that threatens to dominate the popular discussion over autism.

And I, too, sometimes felt a nagging fear that neurodiversity advocates were doing some damage. They used the Web so well to organize themselves, but they also sometimes used it to attack the medical profession or diagnostic labels, and not always in a responsible fashion. Some critics, including members of the autistic community, think they are celebrating their damage to such a degree that they would prefer to have that damage than actually be cured. The autistic blogger Jonathan Mitchell posted the slogan "Neurodiversity: Just Say No" on his site. "A number of high functioning autistics claim that there is a consensus among all autistic persons that finding a cure for autism would be a horrible thing," he wrote. "I long for a cure for autism."

It's not that the neurodiverse as a whole oppose efforts to seek a cure, however. Most simply want to be sure that autistic oddities, skills, and cognitive styles aren't sacrificed in an attempt to eliminate disabling qualities. They distinguish between autism itself and handicaps that can be associated with autism; despite the suspicions of their critics, they aren't all in love with their handicaps.

AUTISM IS A CULTURE

For one of her major works, Katie had two infants lie on a shocking blue shag rug for six hours while she took their pictures and then created a series of paintings from the photographs. She had spent the last three years perfecting canvases of these babies, depicting every fiber of the rug and every red wrinkle of the newborns' skin. While she worked, she tried to obey written signs she had posted around her studio telling her to move around and eat, and reminding her to dress herself in her paint clothes and paint shoes. "While I paint, I have signs everywhere to remind myself to eat, to go to the bathroom, and to stretch," she explained. "Otherwise, I am so extremely focused that I don't realize I am hungry or I have to go to the bathroom, or I only later realize my muscles hurt."

A few times during our conversations at a pizza place, her apartment, and her studio, Katie told me to stop asking questions because she was overloaded. She said this not in the way of someone with a disease, but as someone who felt that the environment—with its noises, its stimuli, its implicit demands that we all must constantly sell ourselves as coherent people and make eye contact—was asking too much of her. The rest of us are often too focused on the kind of personal or financial success that so often requires charming or pleasing others to break from social convention in this way. The neurodiverse offer a critique of social niceties and artifice in their very being: Katie refused to be forced to do anything she didn't want to do.

Two years later, in 2012, Katie had moved out of her home near the art school and was now based in her parents' home in Baltimore County, Maryland, thirty miles north of Baltimore. She still found inspiration in newborns. She also still had trouble meeting men, trouble going to parties without melting down, trouble understanding whether someone is smiling or glaring at her. All of this had made college—and the art gallery scene she later inhabited—a complicated social labyrinth for her to navigate.

According to established biomedical wisdom, the symptoms of autism are always a deficit. Katie and those like her are among the many outsiders who are asking us—perhaps even forcing us, by their own examples—to rethink autism and even what we reflexively think of as "strange" behavior. I, too, have felt odd and out of sync with others at times. I, too, have tried to subdue it, at least as much as I could bear to. But after meeting people like Katie, I wondered why.

The neurodiverse are balking at normalized behavior, at manufactured personalities and minds that align with innocuous consumerism and happy-face aspirations. Thinking differently itself could be a form of rebellion and could get the dominant culture to reassess what is normal—and even what's considered elite and influential. Thinking differently—not just having different ideas, but functioning differently on a cognitive level—has created an autism culture with a demonstrable, thoroughgoing impact on mainstream culture, from Temple Grandin's autism-inflected rethinking of the treatment of animals to a new way of "sharing" that's not emotional but digital: file sharing.

And it is working, at least in a way. Neurotypical people now call themselves "autistic" casually, although not always positively. Often what they mean is that they manifest autistic symptoms, such as being less or unconventionally emotional or obsessing over sets and systems.

Thanks in part to people like Katie, when people talk about "autism" now, they are also talking about a geek ethic. They may even recognize autism culture, something deeply intertwined with the Web: people who are far more alive online than in the so-called real world.

PART TWO

AFTER THE GATEKEEPERS

4

BEYOND HOLLYWOOD

They were close friends when they moved down to the bayou in order to make their film. When the director's truck caught fire, someone in the art department decided to turn the truck into a boat, which became a major prop in one of the film's crucial postflood scenes. Few who were making the sets had ever worked on a normal film—they were simply artists the filmmakers knew. The filmmakers were inspired by pre-computer-age effects and created mythical Ice Age creatures out of baby pigs, training them to wander around miniature environments while in costume and filming them so that they looked like they were twelve feet tall. They didn't use computer-generated imagery because they wanted the creatures to be alive, they said. The fact that they were going against the conventional wisdom of Hollywood was just an added plus.

These young film renegades are Court 13, a New Orleans film collective who together produced *Beasts of the Southern Wild*, a small independent film that, though mythical, conjured post–Hurricane Katrina New Orleans and other southern Louisiana coastal towns beset by storms. It became an outsize hit. To me, the film defines "magical social realism." Part of its success is surely due to its energetic, deeply unconventional nonactors from New Orleans and nearby towns such as Houma. According to the film's co-producer Josh Penn, they cast nonprofessionals because it "felt right to the texture, tone, and fabric of the film." He explained, "They were a degree closer to what the characters were going through." The filmmakers then hung the movie on a six-year-old character named Hushpuppy, portrayed by a local kid named Quvenzhané Wallis. The conventional approach would have been to cast a professional nine-year-old actor in the role, but the filmmakers resisted that formula. Instead, they held extensive grassroots auditions, meeting four thousand girls across Louisiana, speaking to schools and community centers, and distributing flyers across the state. The casting method appeared to be motivated by these outsider filmmakers' obsession with authenticity: a wish to go against the perceived fakeness of mainstream cinema, as well as a desire to put their audience *into* the film.

They met potential adult cast members at bars. If they had a funny conversation over beers, Penn said, they would invite that person to an audition. The lead actor, Dwight Henry, who played Hushpuppy's father, Wink, was a baker. People loved visiting his bakery, so the filmmakers guessed that people in the audience would also fall in love with Henry the baker. "Life experience brings value," Penn added when he talked about Henry and the rest of the cast, all of whom were asked to bring their own lives into their roles.

The characters these ordinary people played were outsiders and rogues, living in a mythical zone called the Bathtub, scavenging crabs and household objects, constantly drunk, partying together in the face of a catastrophic flood. It was shot with a handheld camera on film rather than digitally. It's a shaggy, picaresque film depicting a gang of misfits, truly downtrodden and yet also truly free, trying to survive calamity together. Among a chorus of rave reviews, David Denby in the *New Yorker* called the film "a kind of counter-culture myth," and the film was indeed mythic in content and form. Its free-flowing, noncontinuous storytelling recalled avant-garde cinema of the 1970s. Here are images of inexplicable yet beautiful Ice Age creatures (the aforementioned pigs)! Here is the inexplicable communal party scene where parents act like children and children act like adults! The technique and ethos of *Beasts* grew out of the community art project films directed by Benh Zeitlin, the director of *Beasts*, that Court 13 began making in 2008. "It's a friends-and-family operation," Penn said of the collective. "We had to throw out the rule book and start fresh because we didn't have the budget to do it the normal way."

When Court 13 began work on the short film *Glory at Sea*—a precursor to *Beasts of the Southern Wild*—friends banded together to bring the project to life even while they were constantly running out of money. The crew of forty or even more (Penn could only estimate) moved in together, with everybody piling into a giant dilapidated mansion on the bayou that had been deemed unlivable. They ate mostly ramen noodles.

The process they described was total chaos, an "insane" dangerous adventure, where they would build a boat out of pieces of Katrina detritus from trash piles and then float down the river on it. Some of the producers worked for the 2008 Obama presidential campaign and said they learned from that grassroots operation that you need to give the least professional, most minor-seeming workers a sense of ownership for the projects they made as a whole.

The feature-length *Beasts of the Southern Wild* continued the experience of the grassroots campaign and then grassroots film. They struggled to combine the performances with a taste for surreal, painterly image making, creating a sort of Hipstamatic fairy tale about Hurricane Katrina and edges of Louisiana suffering from coastal erosion. I thought *Beasts of the Southern Wild* was a good example of critic Manny Farber's "termite art": "Termite-tapeworm-fungus-moss art goes always forward eating its own boundaries, and, like as not, leaves nothing in its path other than the signs of eager, industrious, unkempt activity." Farber considered this a high compliment, as do I, standing in stark contrast to the bloated "elephants" of multiplex cinema that he disdained.

Today, membership in the collective is still "malleable," said Penn; it can be "two hundred or four people. It's not a number but a spirit of filmmaking. It's community films, being thoughtful, being good about the places you make them, and having an inclusive process. We are not that interested in top-down things. It's a lie to say there are not hierarchies. But we wanted people feeling ownership for the film, not a team where the director and producers care and everyone else is hired guns—where people on the film set are getting something they feel is valuable experientially."

Months after *Beasts* debuted, many of the hundreds of members of Court 13 are still in constant touch with one another. They aspire to continue making films together. "*Beasts* is not a launching point into making the new Bourne movie," said Penn. They plan to try to stay in Louisiana and make documentaries and fiction films and apply the same mentality to both, hewing to a collective model and emphasizing the Gulf Coast as a destination for local film production. The popularity of *Beasts* was another felicitous counterculture myth turned reality: a gaggle of amateur locals who found an enormous audience that no one would have believed existed. The film was nominated for four Oscars, including Best Picture and Best Director.

Beasts of the Southern Wild is one of many examples of independent filmmakers who carved out new identities, seeing themselves no longer as individualistic superprofessionals, but rather as people defined by and dependent on their fans and the critics and amateurs who create on-screen worlds alongside them. Viewers not only passively watch prebuilt screen worlds; they also engage in creating these worlds themselves, whether by editing digital films on home computers in their bedrooms or by creating a thick Web culture around films. It's as if they are all characters in the Woody Allen film *The Purple Rose of Cairo*—waitresses jumping out of their seats in the movie theater and stepping into the film itself.

Many of the new film renegades—proud amateurs, genre multimedia makers, members of filmmaking collectives, video-sharing documentarians—disdain auteurism or the notion of a visionary filmmaker who works alone. Sure, they have the usual ambition to see their name in lights—or at least on their viewers' laptop screens—but they often reject the cri de coeur of individualism that had shaped popular understanding of great independent filmmaking ever since Andrew Sarris presented his auteur theory in the pages of the *Village Voice* and the *New York Times* in the early 1960s.

There's the *Star Wars*–themed, crowd-created fan film *Star Wars Uncut*, for instance, a loving re-creation of the original *Star Wars IV: A New Hope* scene for scene, shot for shot. Hundreds of people contributed mere seconds of footage, led by a twenty-eight-year-old Web developer named Casey Pugh who lives in Brooklyn, New York. Users became makers, building rough sets (one was made of LEGOs) and casting nonactors—

sometimes schlubby, sometimes hairy—who little resembled the stars of the original. Sometimes the "actors" were actually anime characters or people wearing hand-drawn paper masks. In 2010, the film won an Outstanding Creative Achievement in Interactive Media Emmy, a category that previously had been lavished on websites created by well-paid digital professionals for shows such as *Lost*. *Star Wars Uncut* was different—the independent product of a universe of obsessives who did not know one another and received no pay for their joint labor of love.

On Vimeo, the video-sharing site where users upload their film work, all available in high definition and shown in a player without advertising, millions of films have been finding new audiences. Although Vimeo, which was started by the former CollegeHumor developers Zach Klein and Jakob Lodwick, is now part of Barry Diller's IAC, it also brings together a bona fide documentary community and has become known in the film world as the place to find new, serious short documentaries and excerpts of longer ones or of films in process. The key advantage of Vimeo is that it allows posting films in HD and did so long before YouTube supported the format. It also benefits from strong community guidelines: uploaders have to be the creator or to have participated closely in the creation of whatever they post. If you haven't yet been admitted through the well-bred documentary gates of PBS, it is probably the place for you to move toward that goal. The top documentaries get millions of viewers. Sean Dunne's twenty-three-minute documentary *American Juggalo* obtained 1.3 million views. Dean Peterson's short about a broken subway station stair, *New York City Subway Stair*, got 2 million views and, perhaps more important, quickly led to New York City's Metropolitan Transit Authority replacing the stair.

The controversial Kony video, a short film created by the group Invisible Children to promote the charity's movement against the Ugandan war criminal Joseph Kony, had more than 100 million views on YouTube and Vimeo combined. Tom Lowe, a former political speechwriter and a Gulf War veteran, put his time-lapse film of his desert vacation on Vimeo, where it went viral. One week after he uploaded his first short film on Vimeo, a man across the globe who had seen Lowe's request for funding—which was at the end of his video—wrote him to say that he would send him $100,000 and give him a year to shoot. No longer an amateur, Lowe now makes films full-time.

Such filmmakers often rely on new filmmaking software, cheap DSLR cameras, and video-sharing sites. They hang out at microcinemas, tiny theaters that have popped up around America to show independent films, and have embraced DIY film distribution rather than try to sell their films to established studios.

For some of them, it was a choice not to be film-mad peons chasing the Hollywood dream, but rather a Tarantino of the living room. The birth of YouTube and iMovie and the rise of amateur Web film communities began to alter such fantasies: suddenly people were happily watching microbudget films online. American soldiers filmed elaborate parodies of pop music videos, such as Lady Gaga's "Telephone," featuring a cast of fellow grunts on army bases in Iraq and Afghanistan mouthing the words. There are also horrifying examples of the new power of amateur film: in September 2012, amateur propagandists posted on YouTube excerpts from the anti-Islamic film *Innocence of Muslims*, made by a man using the name Sam Bacile who claimed to be an Israeli American real estate developer; the film sparked riots in the Middle East. (Bacile was actually a Coptic Christian Egyptian American named

Nakoula Basseley Nakoula who previously had been convicted of check fraud and who eventually was arrested for violating his probation.) Such an example made it seem as if the film outsider could nonetheless wield dreadful power. The world at large had become, in the words of Justice Stephen Breyer, a "crowded theater."

FRANCHISING REBELLION

In the past decade, the specialty film divisions Picturehouse, Warner Independent Pictures, and Paramount Vantage shuttered their offices or reduced their budgets to slivers. Money offers for films shown at festivals hit new lows; some distribution companies wouldn't purchase anything. A theatrical market for independent films still existed, but it suffered from the rise of other kinds of technology.

"Traditional film is so capital intensive you either have to be insane or follow a total formula to survive," said producer Ted Hope, an early major player in American independent film, while sitting in his office next to piles of old films stacked like dominos. "Specialized art films have been withering over the last decade." Vital films were being made elsewhere instead, he said. James Schamus, CEO of Focus Features and executive producer of many of the most critically successful independent films of the 1990s and 2000s (he is also Hope's former business partner), told me why there were now *Beasts of the Southern Wild*, amateur Vimeo stars, and *Star Wars Uncut*: the line between film outsiders and insiders had blurred into unrecognizability since his early days as an independent movie executive. He compared the new fluidity in film to that of Natty Bumppo, the central character of the novelist James Fenimore Cooper's *Leatherstocking Tales*.

Bumppo existed in both the world of the white frontiersman and that of the Native Americans; for Schamus, many films today similarly occupy two worlds.

With Final Cut Pro and the like professionalizing at-home filmmaking, the border that once demarcated those inside, who were readily able to create his or own intellectual property, from those outside, and thus traditionally only a recipient of other people's stories and copyrighted dramas, had shifted. Everyone can be a filmmaker; sometimes it seems as if everyone already is.

But what happens when anyone can be a filmmaker? What are the risks of fans and amateurs taking over some of these forms? Not only quality is endangered. Some cultural amateurs and outsiders can be just as or even more obsessed with niche-marketing their work—what I call the "franchising of rebellion"—that they start to resemble Hollywood at its most craven. In particular, one movement that has become a touchstone of independent film, transmedia, has also borrowed heavily from Hollywood, where films have long relied on the promotion of fan clubs and the revenue from movie tie-in merchandising.

Transmedia happens when a filmmaker or a group of filmmakers tells a story across a number of platforms. Henry Jenkins, a renowned media scholar at the University of Southern California's Annenberg School for Communication and Journalism, coined the term in a 2003 journal article, writing that transmedia results when "key bits of information are conveyed through three live action films, a series of animated shorts, two collections of comic book stories, and several video games. There is no one single source or ur-text where one can turn to gain all of the information."

That sounds bravely new and nonhierarchical, even anarchic, lending itself to unconventional storytelling. And often transmedia works do achieve effects that could still be termed renegade or vanguard. The goal is to tell stories in a way that reflects contemporary life with all of its multiple technologies and modes of address.

Yet there's another side to transmedia. Its not-too-distant cousins are swag and action figures. Its antecedent are the Muppets lunch boxes and Luke Skywalker lightsaber toys of my childhood. According to Jenkins's definition, you can't always separate the creative and marketing aspects of transmedia. It can go hand in hand with media consolidation or "synergy"—in other words, it can represent yet another increasingly blurred line between entertainment and marketing. The alt-moviemakers can sometimes seem to accept the notion that creation and marketing are inseparable, that there's a continuum in which a culture product is made, publicized, viralized, and sold.

This concept did not come out of the blue. Its immediate forebear was fan fiction, fictional stories invented using characters from preexisting popular culture. "Slash fiction" is fan fiction that puts those characters into explicitly sexual situations. The *Twilight* books and then film series spawned countless additional fan stories about the same characters and eventually sparked *Fifty Shades of Grey.*

Fan fiction spins out the backstories or side stories of characters in mainstream media, supplying biographical backgrounds, tying up loose ends in plots. People who write fanfic are trying to fill gaps in the existing "canonical" story. The phenomenon of transmedia differs, according to Jenkins, because it frequently is created with intentional gaps and ambiguities, almost as invitations to audience members to fill or spin them out.

A perfect illustration of these contradictions—and a great example of rebel self-co-optation—can be seen in the transmedia efforts of filmmaker Lance Weiler. As a young man working in the film industry in the early 1990s, he spent his days washing down a highway with a hose, over and over again, until finally the road was so slick that it looked like it was made of gray lacquer, a setting for car commercials. He felt he needed the job to get a foothold in the film business, and, like hundreds of thousands of Americans, he longed for Hollywood. He had processed film in his bathtub and taken community college classes in filmmaking.

That all changed with the advent of the Web. He stopped working for Hollywood productions and commercials and started his own transmedia business, Seize the Media. He decided film itself was not the main thing. Rather, he was interested in the question "How can a story live beyond one screen?" Instead of just reviewing Hollywood hits and figuring out how to replicate them, he turned to interactive comics and Second Life, the alternative-reality site, as inspiration. He saw slasher pictures as his models, but he also looked to video game designers. And he turned to his fans to help him promote his films.

When Weiler completed the horror film *Head Trauma* and its companion interactive graphic novel in 2006, the fans of his previous film, *The Last Broadcast*, and people who visited his site, the WorkBook Project, started to do publicity for him. He crowd-sourced all of the film's prints and advertising. Horror fans connected to the film through social networks on Facebook or on Twitter. People would call radio stations on his film's behalf and rally people into theaters. He offered these DIY publicists a full press kit to download and use. Some of them also made their own flyers for the film, as well as fan art: one person created a comic related to the film, called *The Jersey Devil*. He wielded all these connections and coordinated these efforts from a personal computer in Pennsylvania. In 2008, *Businessweek* anointed Weiler one of "The 18 People Who Changed Hollywood." *Wired* magazine described him as the filmmaker who has "been preaching the gospel of self-distribution since the early '90s." He expounds on his ideas regularly in film magazines, yet he refuses to call himself a film director. If you want to know what to call him besides *story architect*, he also likes *culture hacker*—a phrase full of inexplicable promise, glamorously new-sounding.

His cohort aren't "struggling directors" or "film school grads"; they are "culture hackers." "I don't screen films—why should the word *film* define us?" Weiler said. He created *HiM*, a horror story that he describes as a film, a video game, a series of live events, and a graphic novel. He has planned geo-applications for the iPhone and Android platforms that would be connected to the *HiM* "experience." The film itself serves as just one larger component within the whole story world, Weiler said. He and others like him believe that it's important to involve as many people as possible in a film's creation and distribution, in unusual ways, so all of them have an active stake in the film and will promote it; that way films will have a better shot at getting on as many different screens as possible.

While Weiler emphasizes the storytelling possibilities of his method, I couldn't help noticing that concrete examples of his independence had a lot to do with marketing. This wasn't an accident. His tactics, such as letting people develop their own posters or developing movie-specific apps, are also used by major studios. The strategies begun by fans online were so quickly co-opted by major studios that they became a case in point of outsider self-co-optation, and Weiler was quick to start advising studios on the very thing he was doing for his own film community.

When I went to see Weiler and his mob of filmmakers screen their work one night, I knew that the final dream wasn't necessarily to create works of art or to get films distributed in chain theaters around the land (although they probably wouldn't mind if that happened). Instead, they were trying to tell stories across platforms rather than sticking to one and employing alternative means of distribution over traditional ones. They might distribute their films online only or through Netflix. Weiler showed his movies at flash mob drive-in screenings after sending e-mail invitations to hundreds of "friends." The films were projected on the walls of abandoned warehouses for all to see.

Weiler was a contradiction: he was simultaneously truly independent, yet shaped and conditioned by the market. His transmedia Web comics, apps, and indie minifestivals simultaneously repudiate and embrace the most irritatingly promotional elements of the whole Hollywood shebang. Transmedia films needed audiences to make them complete, yet *transmedia* also described the things fans bought to be closer to films: the *Star Wars* action figures, the sippy cups, the branded hoodies.

At an event Weiler hosted for some films he curated, we gathered at a bar and watched snippets from another amateur film, *Universal Record Database*, in which loose-limbed slackers set aggressively offbeat records. A pregnant woman set the record for the fastest licking of a peppermint stick into an edge sharp enough to pop a balloon—after she earned the title for the fastest devouring of 1.2 pounds of food with chopsticks. At the screening, gaggles of homespun ironists chuckled appreciatively as seemingly ordinary people cheered an ex-boyfriend's musical taste, tap-danced, or whirled dollar bills into confetti in a blender on-screen.

"I love your work," one said to another.

The film chicks with dyed black hair and powdered faces weren't into star-spangled blockbusters. Instead, one asked another how she licked a peppermint stick into such a sharp edge in such a short amount of time, recording the interview for her film. What was her candy-sharpening technique?

OUTSIDERS BEFORE THE INTERNET

This isn't the first breakout moment for the film amateur, though. Long before today's millions of filmmaking and videographing outsiders, insistent on representing their vision no matter what, as many as 200,000 filmmakers were registered as amateur filmmakers in what was once called the Amateur Cinema League. Chapters arose around North America, from San Diego to Thunder Bay, Ontario. Members would meet to discuss and screen their films.

This happened in the 1930s. The directors of these films were engineers, salesmen, and former servicemen. Some of the amateur film club members even built DIY projection booths in their houses. Following the advice of books and hobbyist magazines, they tried their hands at freeze-framing and split screens. They showed their films in 16mm (which Eastman Kodak had introduced in 1923 as an amateur alternative to the then-industry standard of 35mm). In film world terms, these filmmakers were all marginal: ordinary people with uncommon passion, experimenting with multiple exposures or scratching film negatives for fun.

In one of these millions of amateur films of that period, a man defied his upper-crust family to romance a country girl. Other films were spoofs of Westerns—YouTube films before their time. Noted experimental filmmaker Maya Deren championed these "amateur" film leagues as a way out of what she saw as Hollywood's descent into mindless commerce. She pointed out that the very word *amateur*, from the Latin *amator*, "lover," means "one who does something for the love of the thing rather than for economic reasons or necessity."

There were other precedents as well, such as the American director John Cassavetes, who in the 1960s and 1970s directed highly personal, existential independent films starring his friends. As his biographer Ray Carney wrote, Cassavetes "ultimately violated everything our culture tells us about movie stars and directors. Watch Tom Cruise on Oprah, listen to a Barbara Walters interview with Meryl Streep, or Charlie Rose. . . . We're all *much* weirder than that." Films such as Cassavetes's—cheaply made, emotionally hysterical, and intelligently talky pictures about men and women on the edge of breakdown—represented rebellious film culture of the time. The Court 13ers admiringly talk about famed yet independently inclined directors such as Cassavetes and John Sayles, who worked collectively on their films with friends and nonactors and stayed true to a small, local style of storytelling.

The earlier incarnations of American independent filmmaking relied on the favor of critics, repertory theaters scattered across the country, and college campuses. They tended to play for a select few in Manhattan, San Francisco, and a handful of college towns. But they formed a set of interconnected small communities, a counterpublic. At these small film palaces you could watch the latest art film, seated on wood chairs that were as hard and unforgiving as the pews of any Calvinist church. The theaters' screens would most likely be torn and the projectors' lenses scratched. These filmic communities treated the common tender of art films as some addicts treat drugs: one met others like oneself and shared the films as if they were a secret high—the works of American Marxist filmmakers after their visit to Cuba in the 1960s; the output of New York City film collectives, like that of filmmaker Robert Kramer, a reporter in Latin America who in 1967 organized a collective known as Newsreel that documented American political activity, such as draft resistance or the famous 1968 Democratic Convention.

"In its heyday, Newsreel tried to make two films a month and distribute a dozen prints of each across the country," according to former Newsreel member Christine Choy. The films would be shown on college campuses, but often "collective members would drive into an urban neighborhood in a blue van loaded with projection equipment and show the film against a convenient wall," Choy wrote in an article for a film festival, "creating an instant inner-city drive-in theater for the masses. The hope was that these screenings would be catalysts for similar grassroots films in the communities where they were shown."

In the 1980s and 1990s, outsider or amateur films often went viral without the Internet. Documentary footage circulated and had an impact way before the Web through now-dead media: mimeographs, public access cable, and videotapes. VHS tapes featuring freaky or countercultural material would circulate underground, like banned substances. Take the seventeen-minute film *Heavy Metal Parking Lot*, about teenage metalheads, or *Shut Up Little Man!*, a viral meme based on two guys who recorded their extraordinarily abusive neighbors' arguments. Such films were passed around on VHS in the early 1990s, traveling via video stores rather than YouTube, Vimeo, or Firefox. Pre-Internet viral culture was more cultish in character partially because, even though it had achieved a kind of exalted status, it was typically harder to obtain. A person had to work to dig it up, back when places such as Mondo Video, Kim's Video, or even Blockbuster were "platforms."

Pre-Web viral culture was more bizarre as it took more effort to become obsessed with the works than it does now. *Superstar: The Karen Carpenter Story*, Todd Haynes's doll-filled reenactment of the life of the anorexic singer, circulated surreptitiously on tapes due to copyright issues over the use of the Carpenters' music. I first watched *Superstar*, made in 1987, in college in the 1990s; my second screening was years later, at a friend's house. I had heard about it by word of mouth and then had to unearth it either at a rarified video store, through a college film library, or via a filmmaker pal. I had no idea that one day I'd be able to watch it by merely firing up a laptop.

Back then—and for decades before—activists, amateur filmmakers, and avant-gardists dreamed of a world where regular people would one day get to make and distribute their own work. The mass of ordinary people should be able to make and share their own cinematic images. The fantasy of American documentary film collectives was that every plebe who thought he or she had something to say would be able to say it on film. Thanks to Vimeo, Twitter, Final Cut Pro, and even the multipurpose laptop, that fantasy of a filmmaking multitude has been realized. But now there are more and more directors competing for fewer and fewer outlets: in 1993, the Sundance Film Festival received roughly five hundred submissions, but by 2008, that number had swollen to more than five thousand, in part because so many film outsiders and amateurs have gained unprecedented access to digital video in the late 1990s. The change in scale makes amateur film culture of the twenty-first century different from older experimental and art-house scenes, primarily in the huge number of people making films and trying to get people to watch them. Now millions of people possess the tools of production. These film outsiders saturate the conventional, established system of film festivals, distributors, and theaters. Their struggle is the struggle for space.

FILM BLOGGERS AS ANGELS

Sometimes the new film outsiders had their victories *after* their films were made, and *Margaret* is a perfect case study of that phenomenon. If you have heard of it, it's not because it was written and directed by the pedigreed Kenneth Lonergan, who was twice nominated for an Academy Award, or because it starred renowned actors who were usually above-the-line talent in television or film franchises, such as Matt Damon and Anna Paquin. Its huge multinational company, Fox Searchlight, did nothing for it. The major film critics from the *New York Times* and *Variety* were not impressed. If you have heard of the film, it is because fans, bloggers, and smaller-scale critics spread the word about the film tirelessly online, especially on Twitter. A small grassroots movement of film renegades formed to save the movie.

On the face of it, *Margaret* started out as more conventional fare than many other vanguard works. It had movie stars, including Paquin as Lisa Cohen, a maddening teen girl who causes a terrible accident and must live with—and self-dramatize—the consequences, and Damon and Matthew Broderick as her teachers.

At a certain point, the film breaks into multiple narratives and becomes the story of civil lawsuits; high school teaching; social class divisions; the ethics of death, mourning, and age-inappropriate romances; casual anti-Semitism and Zionist rigidities; the New York theater scene; opera as metaphor; and unpleasant midlife dating. Characters use phrases such as "moral gymnasium." Overheard conversations pass in and out of audible hearing. The central characters are troubled and troubling. Like certain independent 1970s films or sprawling nineteenth-century novels, *Margaret* tries to accommodate a full world that doesn't always make sense, and it presents all sorts of subliminal messages. It starts with the central teenage character and grows more and more expansive, following other characters as it progresses: the girl's mother, the mother's lover, one lawyer and then another, a group of actors, opera singers. The result is a surprising cacophony that mirrors New York life. Lonergan's idea was that the only way to see the inner workings of society is by representing a multitude of different people, where everyday connections and disruptions torment the film's inhabitants. No comfortable resolution is obtained. The resulting film is messy, overly long, and uneven, yet it has a parable-like power.

Shot in 2005 from a script completed in 2003, the film is also full of allusions to 9/11: mirrored towers reflecting planes, ominous clear blue skies, and cosmopolitans filmed from high above, unaware of how they might seem from the vantage of an airplane or a god. At the same time, *Margaret* is a prickly film about an angry teenager, middle-aged women, and unglamorous death.

But the real difficulties for the film happened after shooting was completed. Lonergan wound up in a legal dispute with a financer because the film hadn't come in at under two and a half hours, as it was contractually required to. He and others (including

Martin Scorsese) recut it numerous times in an attempt to get to a shorter running time. Eventually, in 2011, it saw brief runs in two art-house theaters in its 150-minute running time version. Advertising for the film was undetectable. The resulting terrible box office receipts were not surprising. Structurally, the film seemed fated to occupy an unfortunate space in our culture: that of mainstream work that was demoted to a small indie film and then to something outsider-art-like—abject, forgettable. *Margaret* seemed a damned effort destined for rejection and an early death.

But then the film was rescued by film nerds, buffs, and bloggers—in other words, passionate amateurs, working in conjunction with more established or "professional" critics. The cultural retrieval started toward the end of the 2011 awards season, months after the film had disappeared from theaters. Freelance film critic Mike D'Angelo tweeted that fans should start a petition in favor of getting the film seen. Then the blogger Jaime Christley created just such a petition:

> Kenneth Lonergan's MARGARET opened quietly in New York City and Los Angeles a few months ago, after which it seemed to disappear. (In fact, many major cities in the US didn't get the opportunity to see it at all.) In that time, the film became known as a miracle—a major work of cinematic art, against the odds—to almost all of the critics and cinephiles that were able to catch it during its brief appearance. It has all the earmarks of a grassroots-supported movie phenomenon.

Even before the petition went viral, fans had begun tweeting under the hashtag TeamMargaret. After the petition gained traction, those tweets became a micromovement. According to a critic present at the movement's inception—Ben Kenigsberg, a film critic for *Time Out Chicago*—around November 30 people started to ask about scheduling press screenings in order to bring the film to a larger audience and also make it accessible to viewers who might nominate it for an Oscar or put it on a year-end "best of" list. As a result of the campaign—which included Kenigsberg and others pushing the issue, the petition, and the Twitter horde's tub-thumping—the film became a must-see in London and received encore runs in Chicago; Washington, D.C.; and Nashville, Tennessee. Every day for months, *Margaret*'s followers would extol the virtues of a film that had been buried and written off as a failed experiment. On blogs and all variety of social media, they asked one another and the studio the same question: how can this masterpiece find an audience when they didn't know it existed?

Twenty-eight-year-old Chris Wells was one of these buffs. While working for the independent IFC Center in Manhattan doing promotion, he kept hearing about the film long before he saw it, even though he went to a screening the day after it came out. He had heard about its legendary "six years of post-production," as he put it, and then read the "mixed notices" about the film in the *New York Times* and other places. When he saw it, though, he "loved it; I couldn't believe how good it was." He started talking and tweeting about the film constantly even though it wasn't even showing at the theater where he worked. Wells also kept checking the studio's Twitter feed. "Fox Searchlight didn't mention it once on Twitter, and they have tens of thousands of followers!" he told me. It was as if they were burying the movie and forcing it to fail, he thought. They seemed to want to wash their hands of the whole situation. The film's fans were dismayed by the studio's reticence. "It's a great New York story," said Wells. "It's an accurate portrayal of life in the city, but it transcends that, too."

Margaret then began a second life. "The advocacy of fans and critics online took the place of the ad campaign," Kenigsberg said. "I wrote an article in print that it deserved Oscar consideration, but no one noticed. Meanwhile, multiple people on Twitter conversing with each other about how they all thought the film was great—that had a snowball effect."

Eventually the film got more press as major critics started publishing (sometimes multiple) reconsiderations of the film, augmenting and revisiting their initial mixed reviews. Lonergan released his own three-hour version of the film, dubbed the "extended cut," and in that format it made its way onto the chaotic bazaar of iTunes' Top 100 films, hovering in the Top 50. Screenings of the extended cut sold out. TeamMargaret continued to buzz, exchanging words of praise about the offbeat epic of moral uncertainty at the heart of their community. Their work had turned into a grassroots marketing campaign. Using their personal accounts, Wells and others tweeted about the film, seemingly incessantly. TeamMargaret grew from a hashtag with twenty followers to a group of active advocates who showed up at the multiple screenings that had started springing up in support of the film.

"There's something in the Ethernet or Internet or Twitter or somewhere out in the world called TeamMargaret, [to] which I don't even know what to say," Lonergan said to the Associated Press in response to this legion of *Margaret* fans. "It's like a flock of angels on the horrible computers I despise, out there trying to save my movie."

Margaret was a prime example of how film bloggers and fans could utilize social media to achieve goals. The film had been left by the side of the cultural thoroughfare, but the TeamMargaret film outsiders, working in conjunction with insiders, had sped up the process of 20/20 hindsight and cultural reclamation that in previous eras would have take decades—and, in the case of some works of literature, centuries—to transpire.

Think of the 1927 film *Napoleon*, which pioneered many techniques that later become widely used, including fast cutting. Metro-Goldwyn-Mayer bought the rights to the film and, after screening it in London, cut it radically, changing some of its innovations considerably. The studio then gave it a limited release in the United States, where it was not well received (it was, as they say, set up to fail). The film quickly left theaters and seemingly evaporated from view; it was only truly restored fifty years later, in 1981, after twenty years of work by the silent-film historian Kevin Brownlow.

The film *Heaven's Gate* is an even more instructional example. Loathed and laughed at as one of the most expensive bombs ever when it debuted in 1980, it destroyed the reputation of its director, Michael Cimino, and collapsed the independent studio that produced it. More than thirty years later, the film showed up in a restored version as part of the New York Film Festival's Masterworks lineup, now feted as a classic. Of course, these examples show that traditionally it takes many more years than was needed for the critical rise and fall of *Margaret* to go from scorned or outsider art to esteemed, established work. This process of retrieval of great "outsider" films—often films that were, like *Margaret*, tumultuous, hybrid, and expansive—now can happen immediately, even after a film has been dismissed.

"Films that are plagued by production problems, on-set fighting, and delays gain a certain reputation or stigma," said

TeamMargaret member Wells. Part of what he and the other bloggers, buffs, and smaller critics who championed the film wanted to achieve was to reverse the too-early death and burial of *any* work of art. "The conventional thinking is that if it's on the shelf, it must not be very good. A breed of younger cinephiles wanted to dispute this," he said. "We were well versed in film history; we didn't want to see what's happened to films historically," when they were buried or critically underestimated, "to happen again." Thanks to the Internet, "most of film history is available at our fingertips," Wells continued. "TeamMargaret didn't want to see a great film forgotten."

Margaret did not have to wait more than half a century for its revival. The film and others like it were fortunate to emerge at a time when critical assessment and retrieval of a work could be done in real time by outsiders, aficionados, and amateurs and not just by the critical establishment.

The fans and film bloggers behind the rescue of the film *Margaret*, the Court 13 actors and set designers behind *Beasts of the Southern Wild*, the Vimeoists, et alia—all are proud of their new identities, which lie somewhere between professionals and amateurs, insiders and outsiders. They are citizens of a new sort of amateur republic, relying on themselves and looking to one another, not to Hollywood or only to establishment publications and critics, as sources of information, entertainment, and assistance. They are trying to make their own culture and get viewers to do the same instead of simply being force-fed the big blockbusters from the major studios, films in which the mark of an individual human hand is nearly invisible. The films they make and love aren't delivered from on high. Their makers are at once audiences and creators, fans and stars.

5

BEYOND TOP 40

The title of her album is *Theatre Is Evil*. That's obviously a joke, because singer Amanda Palmer makes aggressively theatrical songs; the most famous ones are about sexism and abortion. Yet for all her aura of independence, she is dependent—not on a label or a manager, but on her hundreds of thousands of fans. That was probably why, during one week in New York City in 2010, she started a show at a large concert space not onstage but on the floor near her audience. She wore gartered thigh-highs and played her ukulele. Her eyebrows were layered in glitter makeup. She talked about e-mails and in-person conversations with her fans. She sang her goth theatrical tunes. She pranced. It was her modernist-high-school-drama-queen thing—*Glee* does *The Caucasian Chalk Circle*—and she never forgot the audience. She told them they should visit her site, tweet about her, converse with her. By singing amid her fans rather than above them on a stage, she showed she was metaphorically both the star and the crowd at once. If that was the case, maybe her fans were rock stars as well.

A year or so later, Palmer was asking her audience for money—a lot of money—because she didn't want to be on her major label, Roadrunner Records, anymore. It seemed that she was aiming to become the face of the future of music, where the artist no longer needed to be a slave to managers and packagers or to the A&R (artists and repertoire) departments of big labels. Rock music has always celebrated the weird and independent, of course, but it has often only paid lip service to these traits and kept their artists tethered to a big industry. Now a self-professed "piano-slayer, ukulele-freak, singer, writer, blogger, lover, freak, co-founder of the Brechtian Punk Cabaret duo the Dresden Dolls" could raise a million dollars from her audience alone. She would have to pay them back, of course, with sweaty shows full of her superfans (some dressed like transgender pirates). In return for dollar bills, Palmer pledged free MP3 downloads. When fans shelled out $5,000 or more, she promised to play a show in their home. The contributors included wealthy artists and an eight-year-old fan who sent her crayon drawings. She told music blogger Tom Quickfall that her campaign convinced her that "we don't necessarily need the old systems that we're all used to in the art world: the way that government art funding works; the way that museums work; the way venues work," and that all of this new outsider fan energy would require a "shift in attitude on the part of the audience where they realize they're actually actively responsible for taking care of their artists and the art." Meanwhile, "artists have to take responsibility for communicating this and taking care of their audiences in a way that they're not used to."

You didn't have to love Palmer's martial anthems or think of her as a bellwether of a notable aesthetic to see this as an outsider victory—a crowdfunding triumph in which an army of fans made Palmer their queen and were repaid in kind with shows in their homes or performance spaces small enough that they could practically touch her piercings.

But Palmer is not only a symbol of the power of fans. She is also a test case of the inequities that can occur when institutions are disposed of but the new citizen-and-amateur model can be misused or has no built-in oversight. Her success wound up demonstrating some of the problems of the fan-funding model when, after using social media to gain fan support and raise money, she then asked for what many found to be simply too much: volunteer musicians who would join her band on tour and work for free. Professional musicians complained that the code of the amateur and the vague fellowship of the outsider had become a fig leaf for exploitation, always a risk in an economy based on *amator* and devotion rather than contracts. Facing sharp criticism for not using any of the $1.2 million she received on Kickstarter to pay such musicians, Palmer reversed course and said she would pay her fans for their efforts.

While the whole brouhaha proved to some that Palmer was callous about economic realities—a goth fat cat counting her lucre—it was actually evidence of a deeper change in culture. Now the "supply side" of filmmakers and recording artists and the "demand side" of fans and new audiences were often interchangeable, with fans and volunteers shaping music nearly as much as the artists do. It was one version of the rise of outsiders and amateurs.

On one hand, Palmer was just taking advantage of the disintermediation—the disappearance of the grinning middlemen who previously connected one institution to another—that the Web has made possible, albeit without much subtlety or awareness. On the other, her case underlined something far more profound: when your money and renown come directly from fans and amateurs rather than another superstructure, the fans may well *be* the artists. The fans who supported Palmer in a sense remixed their relationship to their heroine and to performance. Through their relationship to her and their devotion, they had become professionalized—somewhere between outsider and insider, amateur and trained talent.

The backdrop of the Palmer affair was the sort of murky wallpaper that everyone from stars and producers to bedroom artists and music fans was now familiar with. The traditional music industry had come unhinged; the usual pathways to power and success had been confused or erased altogether. In both realms—thanks again largely to the Internet—it was increasingly difficult to define what terms such as *outsider* and *insider* meant any longer. Who is a fan and who is a star? Who and what is amateur and who or what is professional? It was suddenly all up for grabs. Palmer is an example of the power of fan funding and fan dependence—a way for culture workers of all stripes and activists to move away from big conglomerates.

As *New York Times* music critic Jon Caramanica put it, "The Internet has rejiggered the industry to think differently about star making." The "mainstream cult artist . . . is increasingly what the new model is coming to look like." Reporter Zach Baron, also writing in the *Times*, took the equation a few steps further several months later: "What becomes of the margins when they are, increasingly, just one click away from the center?" The answer to that question was that the "outside" and the "inside" of culture could flow together more easily and rapidly.

In the past, commercial music was selected, packaged, and sold by powerful commercial interests. The A&R and marketing departments of the big music companies functioned as inevitable gatekeepers, which only lucky musicians squeezed past. With astronomical marketing budgets, slick managers, and talent scouts, major labels exerted a kind of informal censorship, shaping popular taste and directing it toward pop insiders they had preselected.

But then, as with so many other media enterprises, the advent of the Web and shareable music files ultimately helped destroy this arrangement. The bottom fell out of record sales, and artists and bands had to rely on tour revenue as the best way to make a living. Overall, CD sales plummeted 50 percent from 2000 to 2010 (although there was actually a smaller drop in CD sales in 2011: they fell 5.7 percent that year, to 223 million). Major record labels struggled to make even a small percentage of their earnings of ten years before. Artists also discovered they could make money marketing their recordings directly, bypassing the large companies completely. As of 2013, there are still plenty of pubescent boy bands, hokey chanteuses, and tinny hip-hop stars racking up album sales and major label promotions, but in terms of physical album sales on CD, there are no longer blockbusters anywhere near the scale of the 1990s or before. (Download sales of single tunes have soared, though.) Person by person, click by click, millions and millions of individual musical discoveries occur on mobile devices and laptops—in hazy, dreamy spaces of mouse movements, scrolling menus, and constantly refreshed recommendations.

And while historically pop fans have always gone to great lengths to see, emulate, and in some cases befriend the performers they idolize, what's different now is the degree to which fans shape what their idols actually make. Many performers now include fans in their creations to an unprecedented degree, so the demand side has entered the production process. Inside and outside can change places when the role of the middleman or mediator has diminished to the point of nonexistence.

To reach fans, it helps to have memorably weird shtick, something that might pierce through all the noise and clutter involved in having such a vast array of music a single click away. Some bands or singers that unmoored themselves from traditional labels came to depend on their intrinsic or self-created exaggerated characteristics, which helped these acts stand out in a cluttered field of easy access. Those acts excelled in what people had started to call an "attention economy," in which a multitude of diversions compete for a diverse audience.

"The digital era makes a little more room for those of us who are interested in outsider music," said Christina Rentz, a representative for the independent label Merge Records, whose roster includes Arcade Fire and the Magnetic Fields. The success of the gently eccentric, existentially minded Arcade Fire is an especially impressive example: their second release, the 2007 album *Neon Bible*, hit number two on the Billboard 200 album chart—no surprise to those who knew that Arcade Fire had built up a substantial following after the influential music website Pitchfork gave their 2004 debut album, *Funeral*, a remarkable 9.7 out of 10 rating.

By 2010, Arcade Fire had continued to expand its audience and sold hundreds of thousands of albums in an era of wildly plummeting CD sales. Their album *The Suburbs* debuted at the very apex of the Top 200, giving Merge its first number one album after twenty-one years in the business.

University of Kansas communications professor Nancy Baym, who studies independent music online, told me that in her research she came across more and more "mainstreaming" of music "that seemed out there." She said, "The quirky and indie have become very successful." For example, the indie band the Polyphonic Spree was instantly memorable because it consisted of anywhere between two dozen and twenty people, sometimes wearing long white robes, all walking and dancing onstage at once. Bands such as Broken Social Scene (which I reported on and spent weeks with in 2005 and 2006) partly sold themselves on their collective nature as a group with nearly two dozen members. Bands might use musical collage, a thick impasto of Xeroxed elements. In these songs, nature was décor, with shamanic elements lurking in the corners, and a lack of a dominating focal point in each musical composition: each bit wasn't subservient to a central theme, as might be the case in a more conventional track. The indie band OK Go's "Here It Goes Again" video featured the band members in a synchronized dance routine performed on a treadmill and became a viral hit: one million people watched it on YouTube in the first six days, and at one point it was the top music video on YouTube. The band has more than 105 million views on its channel, and "Here It Goes Again" is the now one of the 100 most popular YouTube videos of all time. The band gained traction from the video's popularity, and, like so many others, it left its big label and formed Paracadute Recordings. Ariel Pink (née Ariel Marcus Rosenberg), a classic "bedroom artist," still has an eight-track recorder on a shelf in his bedroom, Baron reported, and he and his band maintain their amateur, outsider image. Musicians such as Pink would have been cult artists in the past, exalting in experimentation and obscurity. Now they get the Pitchfork Seal of Approval and sell tens of thousands of records.

"The thing now is to be so outstanding, so remarkable as a singer—so not generic," said Derek Sivers, founder of CD Baby, an online distributor of independent and amateur music. "Your fan is like a red dot, and you the musician are an arrow trying to hit it. If you hit it, you got millions." In other words, the nongeneric or eye-catching or somehow outstanding musician is the one more likely to gain traction in the Web's cacophonous bazaar. Perhaps that explained the rise of successful indie rock bands that seem to bear some resemblance to what is called "outsider art," relying heavily on biographical "outsider narratives." Take Christopher Owens, formerly of the band Girls, who made much of the fact that, though born in Florida, he was raised abroad in the cult Children of God, escaping from the sect as a teenager to live on his own with his sister. Mentored by an oil heir and philanthropist, he wound up with the sort of angelic-looking, vaguely androgynous mien that would please Gus van Sant.

New singers broke down gender barriers as some male singers favored falsetto over using their chest voices. The Brian Jonestown Massacre stood out for its lead singer, Anton Newcombe, who appeared to be certifiable. Justin Vernon, who records under the name Bon Iver, locked himself in a hunting cabin in rural Wisconsin for three months and, with the sparest of recording apparatus and instruments (an old Shure mic, an old Silvertone guitar), made *For Emma, Forever Ago*—dusty, snowy, melancholy, spare, lovelorn music—and then streamed it for free online. Response was encouraging enough for the indie label Jagjaguwar to pick up the album, which eventually sold 130,000 copies, largely thanks to fan sites and file sharing creating a bigger fan base, but also thanks in part to his "outsider" narrative. Having a story line or some kind of gambit didn't mean that the outsiderness wasn't genuine. It was just that these narrative elements were packaged from the get-go or underlined early on when introducing a new act to the public. This wasn't a case of marketing executives imposing a saleable story on its artists, either; these musicians' self- or voluntary co-optation was conscious. As Baym put it, a musician who doesn't stand out has a "filtering problem." "To get attention in such a crowded space it's good if you do it through the appearance of authenticity," she said. "Some of the indie labels I have researched told me they no longer thought of themselves as record companies but as professional attention-getters."

Lots of singers have hoped that hives of their fans could save them over the years. The folk rock artist Jill Sobule raised the $75,000 she needed to record a music project in 2008. Fans from all over the United States and eleven foreign countries sent the cash in just fifty-three days.

Sobule is fifty-two, with platinum-blond curly hair and a speaking voice that's cute and crackly, with a hint of Marge Simpson's sandpaper. "I've turned my stalkers into people who work for me," she said while telling me about the epiphany that led to her crowdfunding innovation. She had realized the world she knew was crumbling three years before, when she was a fortysomething musical "lifer," as she called it. One night, sitting alone in her home in Los Angeles, she decided to try something new. She created a Web domain, JillsNextRecord.com, and posted a request asking her fans to help fund her album. She offered rewards: for $5,000, the donor got a Sobule living-room concert in his or her own home; for $1,000, she would write a song for the donor; for $500, she would mention the donor's name, or another name of the donor's choosing, on the coming CD. She even had her mother solicit for her on her site: "Hi, I'm Elaine, Jill's mother. As you know, my daughter is a real talent. . . ."

After she raised the money, Sobule recorded an album in just one day, with thirty onlookers on the other side of the studio window leaning in. The viewers were not would-be David

Geffens or backup singers or studio muckety-mucks—they were fans who had helped pay for the studio time, the engineer, and the musicians and were present through tune-up, rehearsal, and final recording, having paid anywhere from $125 to $200 for the privilege. Of the many songs Sobule and L.A. punk legend John Doe performed that day, only nine made it onto the resulting full-length album, *A Day at the Pass*, which was entirely fan-funded.

The musicians Steve Lawson and Trip Wamsley have sold enough of their music on the site Bandcamp to make a living solely from its proceeds. (Sobule sells her wares on Bandcamp, too.) Clap Your Hands Say Yeah, an indie band that succeeded without a label, distributed its music itself via its website, and its self-titled CD drew attention from MP3 blogs and got a great review from Pitchfork. The band's manager, Nick Stern, told me a few years ago that "the Web as a form of word of mouth" made up for the fact that "they didn't have a record deal, but they made an amazing record. That is why they were able to do it on their own, so with no licensing, they sold 200,000 records in the States alone."

Independent and sometimes politically radical bands of an older vintage could also sell briskly thanks to the Web and social media. In December 2009, a Facebook campaign by Jon and Tracy Morter brought "Killing in the Name," a then-seventeen-year-old song by Rage Against the Machine, to the number one spot on the UK singles chart as part of the annual Christmas Number One competition familiar to the British public. It was the first time a song had won that honor through downloads alone, and this constituted a strike against the previously ironclad grip on the competition wielded by established pop sources; at the same time, the resurrection of the song had definite political potency. The band and its lyrics were explicitly critical of U.S. domestic and foreign policy, and that 1992 song took on added resonance at a time when the United States was fighting two separate and unpopular wars. Rage Against the Machine had broken up in 2000 and re-formed in 2007. Lead singer Zack de la Rocha gloated over the highly political track's newfound success in 2009, praising how "spontaneous action taken by young people throughout the U.K." could "topple this very sterile pop monopoly." It was also an example of an old song by a band of already popular political radicals finding new power through social networks.

Careers such as Palmer's obviate an older model in which artists had to follow preexisting formulas or obey executives, managers, agents, or other experts. These grandees often told musicians that what they had in mind was not quite right, that there was no market or audience for it. Palmer may not be getting rich from her music—but then, only a select few ever did so under the old system. In the new self-made model, she doesn't have to dumb down her lyrics or squeeze her caterwauling pop songs into three-minute shiny singles with dippy choruses. In return, fans get to sing on Jill Sobule's records or host indie rocker Beth Wood in their homes for living room shows, charging their friends $10. They download tracks offered gratis by their favorite artists to be remixed, worked into videos, or made into ringtones. It wasn't just shtick but genuine ingenuity at work, and it often made for a better product, although such participation could also be read as a co-optation of fans' talents and identities so that the band or singer could triumph.

When Sobule started recording in New York and Los Angeles in the 1980s, she said, "you just wanted to get on stage and sing. The people [from the label] told you when to show up, and then they did the publicity—that's supposedly why you have the middleman. Now, I do a lot of stuff myself—I'm booking my own shows, I am putting out my own records, so why can't I call the club myself? That's easy, I realized."

NO MIDDLE MUSIC MAN

Rock stars were once the lodestones of daily life and collective experience. Popular records spun in bedrooms and dens across the country, and everyone sang along to the radio or the cassettes playing in cars every night.

If you chose instead to be part of a musical subculture, you were resisting that undertow. You were listening, as David Riesman wrote in 1950, "in a context of imaginary 'others'— [such] listening is indeed often an effort to establish connection with them." Fans within these musical subcultures exchanged gifts—mixtapes, bootlegs, badges, and buttons. Perhaps the most famous example of a musical subculture were the Deadheads who followed the band the Grateful Dead on tour and created a gift-based system among themselves. The band's innovation was allowing free tape trading among its followers, which powered the band's success when at first its records didn't sell. Purveyors of alternative music and their fans toured and exchanged records and tapes. They used college radio and an interlocking set of independent labels that could be considered an underground, as Michael Azerrad wrote in *Our Band Could Be Your Life.*

Twenty years ago or so, "alternative music" kids such as me found escape from both their panic and their rapture in morbid, effete, or difficult music. My friends and I made our mixtapes laboriously, pressing Play, Record, and Stop by hand. We went to the dustiest record stores. We handled vinyl records lovingly. When we bought bootleg tapes, we also did cultural math to make sure the band was properly abstruse enough—that our discovery of it, our claiming it, said something good about us, exemplified our rarified tastes, and showed off our pop erudition. Was it imported? Were the lyrics mysterious but literate? At that time I was more often than not dressed in a maple-syrup-colored dress—a shirt, really—and locked in a kind of fugue state, ready to dance to electronica and smoke clove cigarettes, always carrying a Walkman. I thought my precious British bootlegs and my "alternative" band T-shirts represented different kinds of stylish anger or different kinds of too-cool languor. I believed "alternative music" was minor music and more superior for it. It was like minor literature that had been neglected and thus gained value through its scarcity. It demanded aggressive hunting. I tracked down my favorite music and then congregated around it, as if it were a Byzantine icon or a mysterious set of stones worshipped by Druids. As cultural critic Greil Marcus has written, at a certain point in history the quest for leisure turned for many people into the quest for entertainment, and then, ultimately, entertainment turned into a very serious business, almost a religion. When I was visiting those downtown Manhattan clubs and record stores and compulsively making mixtapes more than twenty years ago, I was a devotee of that particular religion. It was an addiction, too: singles were so short they were like sugar high—you went back to the record player over and over again to flick the needle back to your favorite song, now worn into a deep groove. The Internet, of course, extended this ethos: fans organized themselves into Usenet groups long before musicians did so themselves. Such music mailing lists could be considered ancestors of Pitchfork and Stereogum.

In 1999, the singer Aimee Mann, known for her platinum hair and her puckish songs about yearning young women ("For a girl in need / of a tourniquet," as one of her songs went), went against her major label, Geffen, which she saw as hapless and which she resented for meddling with her artistry. Her dispute with Geffen "epitomized the musician's struggle," Tim Westergren, the founder of the Web radio service Pandora, told me. "Aimee Mann was caught in the middle of it." She felt trapped, he continued, though she ultimately proved successful in retaining control of her work despite her label's wishes.

After leaving Geffen, Mann started both her own label, SuperEgo Records, and a collective called United Musicians, which releases others' works; she also sold her CDs through her own website. Founding a label to distribute one's own work was a decision that would become more and more common during the next decade. One of Mann's albums, *Bachelor No. 2 (or, The Last Remains of the Dodo)*, had sold 230,000 copies as of 2008, and her follow-up, 2002's *Lost in Space*, sold 232,000, according to Nielsen SoundScan. She was an early pioneer in marketing herself online, as many musicians would begin to do in subsequent years, including Radiohead, who made a groundbreaking music giveaway offer: fans could pay whatever they wished (including nothing) to download the 2007 album *In Rainbows*. Mann's case embodied the potential for and the freedom made possible by alternative modes of distribution: she felt that her label had failed her and was threatening the integrity of her work to boot, and self-distribution permitted her artistic independence. If she and other musicians could find audiences more directly, they could exercise more control over their music.

Today, the United Musicians site declares that the collective "is founded on the principle that every artist should be able to retain copyright ownership of the work he or she has created and that this ownership is the basis for artistic strength and true independence." This was a declaration that other musicians who had nothing to do with Mann's label or United Musicians would follow.

In 1998, around the same time Mann that was first arguing with her label, a more obscure musician launched a site to help musicians like him sell their music direct to buyers online. CD Baby was conceived as a digital virtual clearinghouse of music by everybody, even rank amateurs, and wouldn't be limited to major-label releases.

When I met him a decade later, Derek Sivers, the site's founder, was impressively personable, impish, and shaved bald as a boiled egg. In telling me how he began the website, he said he was once a frustrated musician, playing in a band he describes as "James Brown crossed with the Beatles." During his twenties, he spent five years submitting his music to musical showcases; despite multiple rejections, he still hoped to get accepted and then go on to a record deal that would bring his music to a broader public. Throughout, Sivers remained remarkably optimistic—even though no record deals were forthcoming—and he still loved being in a band; he would play any instrument but the drums if asked. Like struggling musicians the world over, he spent much of his creative life overlooked (if not outright ignored) by music labels and corporate radio. His sphere was closer to that of poets than music moguls: no limos, no groupies. "There was the sense that there was the Man sitting at the desk, saying to musicians, 'Thou shalt not pass,'" he told me. He decided there had to be a better way.

Sivers set about creating a way to bring his music and other music by possibly obscure, weird, or amateur outsiders—including legions of unsigned musicians—to listeners. He knew the Web was the key, but he wasn't sure how. He came up with the plan for CD Baby: any musician could upload music to the site, which then would make that music available for purchase by anyone. Buyers would be charged for the music—sometimes $7 a CD (and, later, an instantly downloadable MP3 album), sometimes $9. Financially, the scheme would be pro-artist because the site would keep only around half of the cost of the CD, a smaller percentage than a typical label (with the exception of an independent label such as Drag City) would claim.

When Sivers was getting started, it helped that he was an entrepreneur who worked as a computer programmer. He first built the system on his own in his garage. In the beginning he, and eventually his staff, listened to every single album before posting the music for sale. He pledged not to work with distributors or major labels and to sell only music that musicians had sent to CD Baby directly (rather than music submitted by agents or reps for companies). Today, buyers can order music directly from the site, and they can choose to receive the music either as a digital download or as a physical CD (or a vinyl LP) shipped to them from the CD Baby warehouse. For marginal musicians frustrated by the difficulty of reaching an audience, the central clearinghouse offered by CD Baby was a new ray of hope.

Sivers didn't know it yet, but he had started what amounted to a proto-iTunes for indie music. His company attracted both the weird and talented and the weird and talentless. But one of CD Baby's bestselling singers became a major-label star: Regina Spektor, who started out as a conventional girl singing and playing piano. Soon, however, she changed her act. Instead of singing pretty songs about love, she trilled about her tonsils—and found a new audience. In 2004, Spektor signed a contract with Sire Records, owned by

Warner Music Group. Kooky acts and outré gimmicks proliferated on CD Baby; musicians were learning, said Sivers, to set themselves apart in outward, striking, sometimes superficial ways to get noticed out of a now-giant field of musical product.

By 2003, the business was booming. There were a hundred thousand albums on CD Baby. "Ten percent were genius," Sivers said, "and 10 percent were dreadful." A particularly popular genre proved to be "sailing music": nautical or boating songs that try to do justice to, say, 35,000-mile cruises around the Caribbean and the Eastern Seaboard on a thirty-six-foot sailboat. In 2003, CD Baby's fortunes improved even more, along with the fortunes of anyone who wanted to sell music for musical outsiders. To the Apple headquarters in Cupertino, California, three hundred people, including Sivers, were summoned to an event that would change their lives. The group included music managers and publicists; women who had been in bygone punk and riot grrrl bands; and people from dance and electronic labels and the well-known indie labels Kill Rock Stars, Rykodisc, and Matador.

Apple CEO Steve Jobs, clad in his typical turtleneck and jeans, stepped into the scrum. Sivers, for one, felt good: if Jobs was there, rather than some marketing guy, then he must really want to convince the music people to do something. This was a novel proposition. Glittering and secretive, Apple had a cool factor, to be sure, but it was also a gigantic and extremely successful corporation. Compared to Apple, all of these music folks were hoi polloi. Did Apple want to do business with them? Ultimately Apple did. Jobs had come onstage to persuade them to put their music on a brand-new Apple service called iTunes.

"We can make it easy for you," Jobs told them. "It's our goal to have every piece of music ever recorded up on the iTunes Store."

He applied his full persuasive mode to these small independent music labels, which were used to thankless struggles and years of sliding under the corporate radar. Now, rather than being ignored, they were being courted. It was classic co-optation, but the outsiders who were being asked to join a larger entity weren't a minority. They were, in a sense, "everybody."

"Now there's no more doorman or gatekeeper for our music," Sivers told himself. He imagined a bulk data transfer of CD Baby's vast and motley musical holdings into iTunes, and in a matter of months he got many members of CD Baby's flock available on iTunes. He pledged to keep the re-encoding fees down to $40 per album, and fifty thousand musicians sent in checks. At around the same time, sites such as Rhapsody started bragging about the numbers of musicians and tracks they offered. The war was on to be the site with the most artists and the most music. When I met him, Sivers had just sold his company to Disk Makers for $22 million, by which time the company had made $70 million for independent artists and labels by distributing their music.

CD Baby paved the way for previously unknown and unsigned musicians to gain substantial and even large followings without relying on major labels and musical formulas. It was like a minor-league storehouse of independent music, and now iTunes, Rhapsody, and other digital music services carry such musicians as well, along with artists on major labels. With all manner of labels and musicians available on iTunes, the barrier between conventional, insider pop music stars and countless garage bands, esoteric songsmiths, and outsider musicians became more porous. The Man—the musical gatekeeper who had tormented the younger Sivers—had gone into eclipse, at least in some places. Of course, the new Man was iTunes itself.

CD Baby demonstrates both how the Web has changed the very nature of outsider musicians and the paradox created by that shift. Part of the mystique of alternative/underground/outsider music was that it had been hard to find, hard even to know about. But, thanks to the Internet, anyone can access this music now—something they couldn't do in, say, 1990, when I was an alternative-music fetishist trolling for Japanese bootlegs of the Raincoats in brick-and-mortar record stores. By the mid-2000s, "the gates were open for musicians," Sivers said. "'We need more music!' the music websites would tell me."

After spending time with Sivers, I understood how he had managed to persuade a huge number of strangers to put their music on his site without being paid upfront for the honor, and how he then had been able to turn around and sell the site for so much money eleven years later. His success has led to a whole new career for him, serving as a kind of adviser and guru for people looking to become twenty-first-century cultural entrepreneurs.

By 2012, musicians were able to use free or cheap tools online that would have been too costly in the past. The nonprofit organization CASH Music offers open-source digital tools for musicians and labels. Run by Maggie Vail, a former longtime Kill Rock Stars employee and member of the band Bangs, CASH Music explains itself thus: "What WordPress did for bloggers, we're doing for musicians."

Meanwhile, fans were more and more able to remix established artists' music on their own. Bands such as Radiohead routinely made their tracks available for fans to create their own arrangements and mixes, sometimes with astounding results and leading to the release of entire albums of fan remixes. Open-source remixes now abound, from Nine Inch Nails onward. But the line between what was acceptable fan-based appropriation that could, in return, be appropriated back by the musicians was constantly shifting and unclear. For instance, when the Oakland, California, DJ Amplive put out an album of hip-hop remixes of Radiohead material titled *Rainydayz Remixes*, a cease-and-desist order stopped it in its tracks. (The band eventually did allow him to release it free of charge.) But was this encouragement of fellow independent spirits or the co-optation of unpaid labor?

"By ripping media apart and smashing them back together in often unpredictable ways, remixers expose the hidden circuitry" of how we are influenced, Aram Sinnreich, author of *Mashed Up* and a media studies professor at Rutgers University, told me. When this process is sanctioned "by contests encouraging consumers to 'remix' advertisements by their favorite brands, which has become a common marketing technique in recent years," and by label publicists and the like, "where consumers are limited in their choice of audio and video to those clips that have been preselected" and someone besides the remixer has "final say over which remixes reach the public, the chance of genuine critique is virtually nil," he said. In fact, all these remixes and giveaways could seem to be another way of defanging consumer resistance. The "unauthorized" music remix was and is seen as potentially radical, as it tears musical signifiers away from their original context and welds them together digitally with other genres and sounds, producing music that is possibly culturally disruptive or fresh. But the co-opted version of the remix funnels fans' creativity into a star-centered and banally predetermined product.

Examples of both the latter and the former remix were in evidence as audiences remade works by their favored artists and put them to novel uses. Sometimes the excitingly subversive remix was turned into a mere sales strategy. Of course, such use of fans' work, usually for free, could be called co-optation, in that an independent faction is neutralized and assimilated by an established, legitimate band.

A more extreme example of co-optation in independent music is Pandora, which started out as a relatively independent effort to bring music to listeners but was soon glutted with advertising and eventually sold users' data to other companies. It wasn't like that at the beginning. Tim Westergren, Pandora's co-founder, didn't seem like a corporate marketing maven; instead, I could easily picture him running a chain of cafés in Portland called something like Sumatra: an ex-musician, he was airily driven and evangelical about his product, and he told me he created Pandora in part to "save other musicians," especially since record label money for artists had dried up alongside CD sales. Like any musician who didn't achieve full-on fame and recognition, he had long wanted to support the sounds of musical underdogs and, like Sivers, had personally felt marginalized by the insular, hierarchical major label culture of the past. Perhaps Westergren's and Sivers's early struggles as musicians led them to invent sites that have brought listeners incredibly easy access to the kind of music they once made themselves.

Yet during the 2012 presidential campaign, just four years after I first met Westergren, Pandora struck separate deals with the Romney and Obama campaigns to target listeners with requests for their e-mail addresses, although Obama's campaign did not engage in the same fishing for e-mail addresses as the Romney campaign did: for example, a North Carolina woman listening to a Garth Brooks song was asked to supply her e-mail address to the Republican candidate's team. Despite such questionable deals, Pandora remains popular, and I understand why: it was helpful when my baby was bored—the Harry Nilsson channel struck the right chords for my toddler.

SUBLIME, NOT BEAUTIFUL

For fan-funded musicians such as Amanda Palmer, asking people who are already obsessed with them to work with (or for) them has comically and sometimes disturbingly extended their relationships with their audiences. Palmer has transformed them into a cult of personality that could fund her. Of course, it remains to be seen if this equation will keep working. But for now, she and so many other artists have been raised up by the communities centered around them. Their fans, metaphorically, carry these singers in their arms.

But it wasn't just relatively mainstream acts such as Palmer or Jill Sobule who were able to go independent of labels and disseminate their work on their own; so did truly, deeply, madly musical outsiders, like the beyond-world-music label Sublime Frequencies and the expansive yet irked curmudgeon who runs it, Alan Bishop.

"I am pretty private and I don't like people getting into my private space. I'd be a complete fucking fool to do so," Bishop said when I asked him on the phone whether I should come out to Seattle and visit his apartment. Since I wasn't welcome in person, I was left with the more basic details: Bishop is fifty-three years old, lives in Seattle, and chain-smokes. He is a former punk rocker and member of the ethno-experimental band Sun City Girls, which released its music mostly on cassettes, and for a number of years he was a king of the tapeheads.

For three decades, Bishop has traveled around the world recording music from the farthest corners, an outsider ethnomusicologist. The word *cult* attaches to him and almost everything he does. For some bedroom artists and major-label refuseniks, the rebel or outsider aura is something of a gimmick, but Bishop is a more serious example. Part of the difference between the two types inevitably comes down to how much money they can generate and how large an audience they command. Bishop, Amanda Palmer, and some average homegrown rocker mixing his music on his laptop are different in other ways as well. Sublime Frequencies is consistently novel and inventive, as well as rough-hewn and aesthetically chaotic.

The label Bishop started with Hisham Mayet is nothing if not heterogenous. It releases Saigon soul, Ethiopian tribal music, Burmese pop. It has found a small but fervid audience as a label that its site says is devoted to "acquiring and exposing obscure sights and sounds from modern and traditional urban and rural frontiers," in a "global" world where so many like to think there are no boundaries or frontiers left. But most people aren't thinking about music from Bali or Java or Palestine or Libya or Syria. Sublime Frequencies' music lies somewhat out of the matrix of American shopping.

"The label is selfish: I don't want people listening to techno and stupid-ass hip-hop: fuck them," said Bishop, who still retained the aggression and resistance to outside analysis of his punk days. He also had a tendency to make albums in a way few others did and also to be honest about how he felt. "I know what I am doing is right, but I don't have media power to shove shit down people's throats," he said. "The way I put together and put out music means I don't have to deal with the Western industry shit but can provide people with something much superior, transcendent. Not the garbage that music industry makes us listen to."

Sublime Frequencies tries to locate and cross boundaries that Kickstarter stars and indie labels can't begin to define—the bona fide margins—and then to help its sounds infiltrate the ears of the self-centered West. Today, even an outsider musician such as Daniel Johnston, the inventively schizophrenic musician who became famous for handing out tapes of his songs in the 1980s, might not be much of an "outsider" anymore; he might go viral overnight on YouTube singing his great tune "Some Things Take a Long Time." Then, of course, he'd probably be forgotten the next day.

So much of Sublime Frequencies' outsiderness originates in the way the music is gathered, almost as much as what the music is. In one album, "instruments are powered by car batteries and blown out through megaphone speakers." In this context, "raw fidelity" is the highest honorific. The fascination started for Bishop thirty years ago. For his first recording in Morocco in 1983, he used a cheap cassette recorder and recorded live off the radio with a detachable microphone. He was traveling alone, his only companions his saxophone and guitar; he single-mindedly recorded incidental sounds around him, such as calls to prayer.

"I didn't spend more than a dollar or two for a hotel—sleep on the beach or stay with people. I had no clue that it was going to be an album," he said. "I assembled it and edited it, a radio edit on a cassette, and passed it around to friends for twenty years. No one was thinking this would be a cool scene—no one called it 'the cassette trading culture or underground.'"

After Bishop recorded the album *Radio Morocco* in 1983, he went on to make and release *Radio Java* and *Radio Palestine*. The albums included what radio people call "wild noise"—sound from taxis and from the street—as well as "real" music. In addition to being about places that are so often outside the culture that Americans (including indie types) receive, the music's presentation was also vaguely subversive, a cut-up, pastiche-like way that defied concepts such as "album" or "song."

From the beginning, though, this was an explicit rejection of the notions of popular and world music that musicians such as Paul Simon mainstreamed in the 1980s, trying to lure Western audiences by mixing in American pop. That music might be heavily produced, or it might try for something more archival and folkloric, as Smithsonian Folkways does or as the great American folklorist Alan Lomax once did. Sublime Frequencies is also something of a refutation of the latest, coolest remix of "world music" by M.I.A. (given name Maya Arulpragasam). M.I.A. samples music and sound from the corners of the world in music that becomes Top 10 anthems and music for Honda commercials yet is also music, somehow, about violent revolt. The London-born Sri Lankan, a former art school student, may be either a revolutionary or a sellout, wrote critic Joshua Clover. The poncho-wearing cliché that clings to world music, the polished *Music of . . .* albums, M.I.A.'s radical chic: Sublime Frequencies rejects or augments these norms. It has for all these years remained simultaneously subjective, hybrid, and obscure—and proudly below the radar.

The label issues only a thousand copies of any given CD, which frequently sell out, ignoring the fact that MP3s are a nearly infinitely reproducible format. It's curatorial in a way that marries the selection process of documentation of past folkways with a weirder, more naive sensibility that has more in common with Internet aggregation than with ethnomusicology.

That said, Sublime Frequencies is full of some of the same para-
doxes as Paul Simon or M.I.A.: what are the politics of taping
quasi-anonymous musicians of the developing world or doing
heavily curated albums full of radio samples for the delectation of
arcane American fanboys?

Sublime Frequencies began when Bishop, Mayet, and other
compatriots began meeting twice a month for a while and deter-
mined they had so much recorded and found-sound material that
they should just start a label that would draw from their huge ar-
chive. "Other labels didn't seem interested, so we decided to start
a label based on our collection," said Bishop. "There's no tem-
plate. Whether or not we speak the language is never an issue. I'd
go on a tour, playing music, and I'd record. I've used a phone to
record on occasion, but usually, for better fidelity, audiocassette
with microphones and equipment I've found on-site, including
cheap video cameras." At the time, their sound collection consisted of albums, films, and radio collage—retro music from cassettes, tapes, and field recordings covering a fifty-year span and a
wide geographical range, from North Africa to Southeast Asia,
from Burmese vintage pop by a singer named Princess Nicotine
to the sounds of Thailand's psychedelic "ghost festival." In 2003,
the label began releasing the material they had been recording
and collecting for years.

Sublime Frequencies has functioned for ten years on the kind-
ness of a "complicated system of friends," as Bishop called them,
but has just barely managed to pay for production costs, for some
travel costs, and for helping to fund their artists' tours—although
the authorship of each song they release is not always so clear, as
the songs come to them in such roundabout ways. "As you get
even older, it gets weirder, but older is better: things reveal them-

selves to you," he told me, with an air of mystery. During one of our conversations, he added, "I am out there, man! Come on, I don't need publicity—I am talking to you because I am bored." His public self could be considered nothing more than an outcropping of his boredom, if that was in fact why he was consenting to publicity, ensuring that he straddled the line between cultish and absolute outsider. He was indeed cultish, written about in small magazines; everyone from computer programmers to an abstract-jazz drummer I know nodded assent when I mentioned the label. But Bishop was close to a true outsider in the way he went about his business. Whenever I spoke to him or mentioned Sublime Frequencies to enthusiastic initiates, the label and its obscurantist fans seemed to be the very definition of a subculture, a term that emerged in the 1930s and became popular in academic writing around 1945. (I've used the word *subculture* elsewhere in this book—and deservedly so—but, with all due respect to cultural studies professors who insist the sobriquet is dated and useless, Sublime Frequencies is a classic example.) In the first half of the twentieth century, subcultures were often thought to incorporate large parts of the culture at large while breaking from that broader culture, sometimes in extreme ways. In 1950, sociologist David Riesman wrote that a "subculture . . . actively sought a minority style" and "interpreted it in accordance with subversive values." In late 1970s England, scholar Dick Hebdige defined "subcultural style" as something that individuals "fabricate," unlike mainstream style, which he considered prefabricated, ready-made for the consumer. Appropriate to the period when Hebdige wrote his canonical book on the subject, *Subculture: The Meaning of Style*, his subculture of choice was punk. Punk defined itself by borrowing objects from "the most sordid of contexts," he wrote.

For Bishop, the contexts that he borrowed from were not sordid, but they were far-flung and often abstruse to Western ears. Unlike many other renegades mentioned in this book, he was not courting publicity: he was so hard to track down online that I wound up calling for him at a Seattle record store where he was a well-known eminence. "I want to turn other people on to the things I like rather than the things other people like, for the world to be influenced by what I personally like," he explained.

Bishop, his label, and his artists were so independent that they didn't seem terribly interested in new independent-music conventions such as fan funding, to name one. So many American subcultures were intimately linked with specific locales and dependent on expanding technologies that I couldn't help but wonder if the microresistance of a label such as Sublime Frequencies, with its disinterest in crowdfunding boosterism and its international scope, could be an index for the future. What if "the hipster" was finally laid to rest as an empty signifier in too-tight jeans, readying Americans for a taste of cultures that were more global and less techno-cheerleading? In the case of Palmer and so many others, the methods of reaching people were new, but the music was appealingly familiar and sometimes predictable. Bishop, on the other hand, was not raising a million dollars or even hundreds of thousands of dollars from fans, and had gone far afield from the "outsiderness" of a figure such as Sivers; his label's music wasn't even sold on iTunes.

The price he paid for not eagerly marketing and selling his difference was, obviously, sales—and sometimes also influence. But he had gotten rewards nonetheless. "I am making my own reality," he said, "making things up as I go along."

PART THREE

THE CENTER CANNOT HOLD

6

BEYOND MEAT

David Lee liked to ride his bike down to the International District in Seattle, the neighborhood of Southeast Asian businesses and restaurants sometimes called "Little Saigon." He passed factories, Thai and Laotian restaurants, and a chicken slaughterhouse on one of the smaller streets. As a professional chef, Lee was particularly drawn to the poultry plant, but for weeks he couldn't work up the courage to go inside.

Then one day Lee passed the slaughterhouse parking lot and saw something: a chicken dying on the ground. It had either escaped or been dumped there, he thought. His eyes went to the emptied trailer the chicken must have arrived in, which was parked nearby, and then to the bird on the ground, forgotten, half alive. He went up to the dying bird and thought: look at the lack of dignity. He knew that what he was seeing was generally regarded as just what happened when you worked with live animals: a small percent of animals raised in industrial farms die being transported.

After half an hour or so, Lee had to leave for work, and he got back on his bike. It bothered him for weeks, though—a trauma flash amid the gray hills of a city. The memories of the bird, bleeding and dying, returned to him in quick crackly bursts, as if filmed in Super 8.

After seeing the dying chicken in the parking lot, Lee went on a formal "chef's tour" of a slaughterhouse, with the belief that he should see with his own eyes the entirety of the situation that produced the food he cooked. Before he entered the plant, he passed through the parking lot again and saw trucks stacked with cages full of animals. At the plant's entrance, he saw the chickens being off-loaded. When he went inside, he saw them pulled out of their cages by their feet, onto rolling conveyors, then watched their feet bound to a moving rail before being dipped into water; they needed to be wet so they could be properly electrocuted. The slaughter would continue when a little V-shaped blade caught their necks and cut their heads off. But sometimes the blade didn't do the trick, and the chicken, still fluttering, started dying slowly—and we can assume painfully—until a man called a "sticker," working alone, finished the job with a V-shaped knife. Lee called the sticker's job "the loneliest on the planet."

The slaughterhouse tour was Lee's final epiphany. He decided then and there to leave the job where he cooked meat. He would cease to be an earnest but carnivorous chef and instead become an animal-rights true believer—a vegetarian who sometimes ate fish and, eventually, a vegetarian entrepreneur.

ANIMAL RIGHTS LITE

Today, Lee, fifty-three, spends his days producing meatless sausages made of grain and apples. He wants to make faux meat the center of the plate for American consumers. In 1996, a few years after his horror over the slaughtered chickens, Lee decided he wanted to make vegetarian meat. He developed product after product in his own kitchen by himself, taste-testing as he went.

Lee began the company Field Roast with $5,000 of his own start-up money and $5,000 from his brother, with more money raised from friends, family, and employees' families. Field Roast makes and sells only "fake meat": nonmeat sausages, nonmeat meatloaves, and nonmeat luncheon meats. By 2009, it was bringing in $3.3 million in annual earnings, with sales increasing 50 percent a year, according to Lee, a Seattle–nice guy in a fleece jacket, occasional cravat, and mane of white hair. While his company was small fry in terms of overall sales compared to other food manufacturers, he was a good example of how a once-outlier stance such as animal rights had become one so commonly held that it was encountered every day, at least in some parts of the country.

In his small way, Lee is part of the rise of animal rights. In his version, though, being an animal rights renegade is more fun, cheaper, and more accessible than in the past, or is repackaged as such. More and more, the phrase *animal rights* has been replaced by the more benign, curatorial *animal protection*, likely chosen to sell Americans on a subtler-sounding, less wrathful movement, offering fake meat instead of guilt. It is typical for an outsider seeking to cross over to the mainstream to use language that makes the abnormal seem more normal—or, as legal scholar Kenji Yoshino puts it, "to cover." Lee and others like him are trying to redefine the word *meat* so that it no longer means "animal flesh" but "any solid food." (Lee chose the name Field Roast, he says, to connote "flesh of the earth.") A newer, more intellectual term, *animal pragmatism*, further softened the movement's brash, contentious legacy. While *animal rights* no longer necessarily conjures images of protesters throwing paint on fur-coat-wearing women or annoyingly pious hippies worrying that honey is exploitative of bees, *animal pragmatism* encompasses fun cookbooks with names such as *Veganomics*.

Lee's employees are, of course, not carrying V-knives and slitting the throats of chickens. Instead, Field Roast's "vegetoir"—a vegetarian abbatoir—looks like a nightclub in the 1990s, with an exposed wood-beam ceiling and brick walls housing Hobart mixers and Bizerba sausage slicers. I walk with Lee as his boots tread carefully on the wet, red-painted floors, his shock of lush white hair covered by a protective hairnet, while workers put dough through the mixer and then into ovens, mixing the batter for breaded cutlets with ingredients including hazelnuts. Lee gives me a sample: it isn't at all like the dry and desiccated vegetarian meat I've bought from the supermarket. Field Roast has good "mouth feel," Lee says—a technical term for the texture of a food when it hits the consumer's palate. His "meat" was spicy, salty, juicy, and surprisingly fatty—and, of course, sold at Whole Foods.

Lee labels the grain sausages produced by his vegetoir "vegan grain meat." They are aimed both at vegetarians and at so-called flexitarian consumers, who eat meat occasionally but eat meat substitutes more frequently. He isn't the only entrepreneur to target the growing vegetarian market as well as its more flexible variant. According to a 2008 study commissioned by *Vegetarian Times*, 3.2 percent of U.S. adults, the equivalent of 7.3 million people, adhere to a vegetarian-based diet. While only 1 million Americans are vegans and eschew all animal-based foods, including dairy, eggs, and honey, 10 percent of American adults follow a flexitarian diet. According to the food and beverage market research group Innova Market Insights, more than 44 percent of American eaters ages eighteen to twenty-nine eat a meatless meal at least once a week. A movement that once was associated with fierce animal rights activists has come to include the occasionally vegetarian, organic lifestyle of the middle class (and well-bred novelists). Due to the rise of vegetarian burger sales in America in 2011, meat burger sales dropped. And vegan foods aren't restricted to places commonly associated with vegetarianism—Field Roast is sold at Costco, for instance. More and more companies like Field Roast are trying to get nonvegetarians to try their products. In 2012, a new product called Beyond Meat, which was supposed to even more closely emulate the real thing, was introduced. The company received funding from a Silicon Valley venture capital firm and was trying to get stores to stock its "meat" at the actual meat counter, near the beef. Its founder told *Slate*, "Our goal is to see that category redefined— instead of having it be called 'meat,' it would just be called 'protein,' whether it's protein coming from a cow or chicken or from soy, pea, quinoa, or other plant-based sources." Beyond Meat also costs as much as actual meat products.

Beyond Meat, like Field Roast, is an example of Animal Rights Lite. On a larger scale, you can see the effect of the mainstreaming of Animal Rights Lite, its rhetoric becoming a publicity tool for enormous carniverous conglomerates, in Burger King's 2012 announcement to "transition" in the next five years to eggs from cage-free hens and to pork from suppliers who refuse to use gestation crates for pregnant sows. By 2012, even McDonald's was swearing up and down that the future hamburgers of the world were being treated humanely. Companies from Quiznos and

Kraft Foods to Starbucks, Carnival Cruise Lines, and Sara Lee are also on the road to transitioning to cage-free, according to the Humane Society of the United States (HSUS). The same effect is even at work in a bottle of nail polish I bought: the little rabbit on the label promised me it was a "cruelty-free brand and is committed to ending animal testing."

Today, big supermarket chains aggressively market an image of themselves as moral custodians of industrial animals, frequently decorating their meat counters with soothing images of happy, blue-sky farms where contented animals roam without a care. Such images create an illusory atmosphere that writer Michael Pollan has branded "supermarket pastoral." The organic superstore chain Whole Foods decided in 2000 to investigate the welfare of the animals it eventually sold as meat. The company examined a number of potential methods for animal protection and then, in 2007, turned to animal-welfare scientists to set up a list of basic standards for their animals: no growth hormones and antibiotics; increased attention to each animal's daily physical welfare so that it wasn't, for example, sleeping on wet straw or in cramped, unhealthy conditions; no gestation crates for sheep or chickens. In all of these cases, a combination of good intentions and superficial sales methods were at work. "There's so much unrest in the world at large that people are thinking about their food and they can't help but being aware now," Margaret Wittenberg, global vice president of quality standards for Whole Foods, told me. "Once you know how animals are raised, you have to do something. . . . My life quest is improving food sources. If people had the opportunity to know more and more transparency, people would be able to make better choices."

The meat aisles of Whole Foods and other stores proclaim their happy-meat awareness. Whole Foods' five-step animal-rating program, which rated how pigs and cattle had been raised before being brought to market, served as a would-be Geneva Convention for creatures on four legs. The program was painstakingly detailed both on handouts in the store and on its website. The rib rack and veal in the display cases bore labeling that claimed the animals had been raised and slain kindly. Multiple proclamations of the decency with which the animals were raised—their lives had been "barn roaming," "free ranging," or "free farmed"—proliferated throughout the meat and poultry cases. The store no longer sells live lobsters, floating in tanks with their claws in criminals' handcuffs. Now there are neater, more seemingly rational labels on our meat, such as "animal compassionate" or "certified humane." (What kind of treatment qualified as "compassionate," though? The truth was often hard to untangle.)

Eating "good" meat can, of course, be interpreted as just another variation on the traditional relationship people have had to animals, which historian Diane Beers, author of a history of the animal-rights movement called *For the Prevention of Cruelty*, characterizes as "consumption, consumption, consumption." Field Roast and Beyond Meat tell the consumer that, with a slight change of habit, such as buying sausages made from grain rather than pigs, you, too, can participate in animal rights.

These new nonmeats are a far cry from the more radical early days of veganism and animal rights, though the more extreme wing of the movement still exists and could be said to take an abolitionist position for which no happy meat suffices. For Lee and others like him, it's enough to just get people buying a little differently; that in itself is a win for a formerly marginal movement. But is acceptance of animal rights via flexitarianism and shopping at Whole Foods simply a deluxe assimilation of a hard-line movement into an easily digested lifestyle? And if so, is it partly the inevitable fate for outsiders who succeed?

The mainstreaming of the animal rights movement also has something to do with the Internet, of course. In the last ten years, vegetarians (often quite pretty) started filming and distributing their personal apologies for animal suffering. With the free circulation of such videos online, these testimonials made an intervention in culture that had been unavailable just a decade before. People started posting an increasing number of amateur slaughterhouse videos on YouTube. Video-sharing sites made activists' message vividly, and sometimes nauseatingly, unforgettable: a wide-open (or almost wide-open) virtual speakers' corner for the rough-and-tumble play of this and other special-interest groups.

Slaughterhouse videos were so sensational that from time to time they would be covered in mainstream media. People for the Ethical Treatment of Animals (PETA) slaughterhouse videos in particular became legendary on YouTube, some of them so outrageous or disturbing that the site has shut down PETA's channel on occasion. (Founded in 1980, PETA agitates for animal rights and vegetarianism and is well known for using celebrities and sexualized imagery to promote its message.) Before YouTube and similar sites existed, few people outside the food industry ever had witnessed the industrial slaughter of cattle, but now anyone with an Internet connection could watch a cow actually being killed. Slaughterhouse videos soon became a genre unto themselves: they were usually taken surreptitiously, via hidden camera, by self-appointed spies or saboteurs of industrial meatpacking. The thrill of the stolen, the frisson of access to the sight of the forbidden—

and of being present at the scene of the grisly crime—pervades these often grainy, muddy videos. Gabriele Meurer, a veterinarian who worked as an official for slaughterhouses in England and Sweden, became a heroine to the movement for smuggling out videos of the industrial slaughter of cattle.

Animal rights videos weren't limited to presenting horrifying images. On his personal YouTube channel, Johnny Durham, a vegetarian and clothing entrepreneur, posts affable, closely reasoned arguments in favor of vegetarianism. He's British, he's charming, he's pretty, and he knows it. Wearing a T-shirt that says "Meat Sucks," Durham, his face softened by deliberate overcontrast, tells his 194,840 viewers, "Every time you're eating any dish with meat in it, you are directly responsible for the slaughtering of an animal." Brittany Roberts, a Boston art student whose *nom de vide* is Tofu Guru, runs a small network of blogs and YouTube channels through which she demonstrates recipes for vegan lasagna, vegan chili, and a 100 percent vegan Thanksgiving feast. Her segments resemble five-minute Food Network shows written by a slacker Hollywood screenwriter: she apologizes for forgetting to put tofu ricotta on one layer of the lasagna while peppy indie rock plays in the background.

You could read about animal rights in bestsellers that simultaneously reflected and transformed popular attitudes: Pollan's *The Omnivore's Dilemma*; Eric Schlosser's *Fast Food Nation*; Jonathan Safran Foer's *Eating Animals*, a personal jeremiad against meat eating and factory farming; *The Face on Your Plate: The Truth About Food*, in which Jeffrey Moussaieff Masson described his own conversion to veganism. The success of these books signaled the movement's drift out of the fringes and toward the mainstream.

The triumph of Animal Rights Lite can be seen in things such as the rise of soy milk, which had $924 million in sales in 2010 and $846 million in 2011, or fast-food joints from Denny's to Red Robin serving "vegan patties." (One supermarket trade journal nonetheless insisted on calling buyers of veggie burgers "special-needs consumers.")

Animal Rights Lite is a case study of a more general absorption of a subculture by the mainstream. Its acolytes affably offer reasons to consider not eating meat and thus join a very cool community with great T-shirts. To participate, you could watch the popular documentary film *The Cove*, which exhorts us to save dolphins, or buy a pair of leather-free Mary Janes designed by a starlet. Perhaps the ultimate example was when, in 2011, 378 staffers and Oprah "went vegan" for a week. Oprah's vegan diet represented both the wider influence and the conquest of an alternative movement. The "choices" were simultaneously real—millions of people were encouraged not to eat animal products for a whole week—and just gestures. People were certainly absorbing some of the messages of animal rights and had become newly mindful of the potential ethical importance of what they eat and what they wear, and of how their lives and choices affect other living things. But are these new choices just offering us different ways to spend money and feel good about ourselves? Or are they of a changed way of thinking thanks to an effective subculture?

The answer is both. Animal Rights Lite has succeeded because it offers easier solutions than storming animal testing laboratories. In a sense, it asks to be co-opted. It would be so great if the mainstream went vegan, it says; yes, we can go à la carte with your ideals. Its recipe for renegade success promises consumers that they can have their (imitation) lamb and eat it as well.

ANIMAL RIGHTS HARD-CORE

Steven Wise, a lawyer living in Florida, is not interested in Oprah's experiments in veganism. He is an old-school renegade, an animal rights purist. Wise's visits to a restaurant can quickly turn into epic struggles to avoid animal products; he orders a plain bagel and tea at a deli, telling the waitress twice to hold the butter. He taps his feet, clad in black lace-up shoes made of plastic, not leather. He is a close talker whose face reddens with passion when he discusses the plight of his unusual legal clients.

As a plaintiffs' lawyer, he represents victims—but not those suffering lead poisoning, violent crime, or injury on the job. His clients are dogs, cats, and other animals. The author of the book *Rattling the Cage: Toward Legal Rights for Animals*, Wise is a renowned animal rights lawyer. In the classes he teaches at Harvard and the University of Michigan, he argues against the legal status of animals as things. Monkeys, for example, have a right to personhood, he argues, and then he asks about animals' moral and legal rights more broadly.

Ten billion farm animals are killed each year for food in the United States or raised for eggs and milk; 56 billion land animals are slaughtered globally. Most are killed neither carefully nor gently but are raised and maintained under harsh conditions; as of 2012, 90 percent of all American egg-laying hens were still kept in cages, according to the Humane Society. Despite increased awareness of the cruelty involved, the number of animals slaughtered in traditional industrial fashion is growing, not decreasing. In 2007, the world ate an estimated 284 million tons of meat. According to the FDA, Americans consumed around 138 pounds of meat per person per year in the 1950s and 195 pounds per person per year in 2000. The global meat market is supposed to double before 2050 and has already expanded dramatically in developing countries. In advertisements, pink-fleshed beef or bright red lobsters are associated with happiness, satisfaction, and prosperity, with providing well for one's family. Yet antibiotics are fed to herds or flocks to induce rapid weight gain. The Humane Society has made a point of highlighting how downed cattle (cattle too ill, old, or terrified to walk) are killed at meat-processing plants that serve the school lunch program; the video has been viewed more than a million times. Humane Society representative Wayne Pacelle lamented that these debilitated animals "are going onto the plates of children."

For Wise, it all started when he first read Peter Singer's 1975 book *Animal Liberation* in 1982 and, in short order, became a vegetarian and one of the first animal rights lawyers. In that famous book, Singer wrote that both humans and animals suffer, and that if we ignore animal suffering, we are "speciesists." We imagine that humans possess superior moral status by virtue of our higher reasoning, and we think we are entitled to exploit or abuse animals because of this presumed superiority—yet that entails a contradiction, as our willingness to exploit and abuse weaker beings lowers our moral status. While the actual treatment of individual animals was a serious ethical issue, according to Singer, his most unsettling, boundary-busting claim was that we shouldn't draw an ethical line between humans and animals at all. Reading *Animal Liberation* changed Wise's life.

His first major case was in 1981. Wise defended a group of small donkeys called burros in California against U.S. Army killings. In his book, Wise wrote that the U.S. Naval Weapons Testing Center in China Lake, California, "had shot and killed over 600 feral burros and they were planning to shoot another

500 starting on Saturday morning. They would keep shooting on weekends, until they killed 5,000 burros. I wasn't altogether sure what a burro was, but 500 of them would be dead if I didn't do something . . . fast." The case dragged on for eight months while he and his legal team "bargained, negotiated, cajoled and ultimately settled the case, so that not one more burro would get shot."

Wise objects to animal protection law as it stands today, arguing that it's no more than an extension of nineteenth-century human slave law. He told me he had sought legal personhood for members of the ape family due to their mental similarity to humans. (A similar case was made in Spain in 2008, when its parliament passed a law granting human rights to apes.) Such creatures have legally protected interests and should have these interests defended, even when they conflict with human interests, he argues. He said this loudly to me in the middle of a restaurant, his square glasses slipping down his nose.

"Why should we always give humans a legal advantage over animals?" he nearly shouted.

Although many of his cases get thrown out, he remains firm. "I decided to fight the practice of animal slave law against nonhuman animals," Wise said. He then added, at the risk of sounding offensive, "I'd do the same things for a [human] slave!"

Twenty-five years ago, calling animals "clients" and specifying that they were "nonhuman animals" rather than chimps or bonobos was considered pretty wacky. At that time, few if any law students chose to focus on animal protection law, partially because it wasn't taught in law schools. When animal protection law—or "animal slave law," as Wise put it—began to become a specialty, Wise was frequently humiliated for his beliefs.

Opposing counsel once barked at him (yes, like a dog) when he entered a courtroom at the beginning of his career.

Nonetheless, animal rights law started making inroads: twenty-two state and local bar association animal committees and ninety institutions—among them New York University and Harvard—now offer instruction in the field, and there are three law journals dedicated to animal rights. Major white-shoe law firms now take animal rights law seriously enough to offer their services pro bono for legal cases centered on the issue. But Wise still bore the marks of that early humiliation and aggressively pushed his views as if sure he was about to be mocked or shouted down, as if he still expected to be woofed at when he walked into a courtroom.

The animal rights' lawyer's truest ancestors lie in nineteenth-century social movements such as utopianism and abolitionism. Beers sees present-day animal rights as part of a lineage that includes the starchy Philadelphian Caroline Earle White, the founder of the American Anti-Vivisection Society, among others. White started her career as an animal-rights activist in 1866, when she worked to establish the Philadelphia branch of the Society for the Prevention of Cruelty to Animals. One of her innovations was the idea of sending telegrams to animal-protection advocates and federal officials when a person saw that an animal had not been fed or watered for twenty-eight hours or more while in transit. Using the cutting-edge technology of the time to communicate rapidly, she and her fellow renegades convicted a number of animal owners of cruelty. More importantly, they spread the very concept of "cruelty to animals."

Back then, animal rights and animal suffering weren't typically part of the public debate. Ordinary people often thought

White insane. Her society had to figure a way to create awareness out of whole cloth. From the beginning, they showed inventiveness and technological savvy that seems somehow familiar. They circulated shocking photographs of animal cruelty and butchery. They wrote articles describing seal hunts in gruesome detail. Activists caused traffic jams in New York City when they protested cruelty against workhorses on the streets. When they alleged cruelty at P.T. Barnum's shows, they got the impresario arrested. They went undercover in labs to expose cruel acts of vivisection.

It was in the nineteenth century that the United States' earliest animal-rights groups realized they had a diverse agenda—and, rather than try to tame it into a single message, they embraced the heterogeneity. (Something similar happened at the same time with the nascent women's movement, whose members were even more at odds about its meaning and direction.) Outsiders who worried about animal welfare saw that their efforts could go in any of a number of ways: Protect work animals? Protest slaughterhouse conditions? Help strays that typically were rounded up and drowned?

From the beginning, there were also some vegetarian appeals to morality that rivaled the abrasiveness, absolutism, and irritating self-righteousness seen in their modern-day animal rights counterparts. Consider Fruitlands, the commune in Massachusetts started in 1843 by Bronson Alcott, perhaps the most famous vegetarian activist of the mid-nineteenth century. The father of *Little Women* author Louisa May Alcott, Alcott devised what he called a "Pythagorean diet"—no meat, eggs, butter, cheese, or milk—and forced his family and disciples to follow it. His refusal to eat meat was grounded in ethical reasons, and he chose to feed on apples and other food from the commune's orchards. He also postulated that a nonmeat diet liberated women from the kitchen. "Man debases himself by his use of animal food," he preached. "There was no butcher in Paradise." Fruitlands embodied the frustratingly Spartan aspects of a fringe movement. The strict fruit-and-grain diet was so limited and the amount available to members was so lean that some suffered from malnourishment and left the society before it collapsed less than a year after it had begun.

As the decades passed, veganism took on a broader life. In the twentieth century, some vegan products succeeded as a result of clever marketing: in the 1930s, soy juice began to be called soy "milk," which was much more appealing and familiar-sounding to the American consumer. (Dairy farmers lobbied against the name *soy milk* because they understood how much damage that product might do to sales of cows' milk.) The interest in eating ethically came as a response to the rise of meat consumption and the mass production of meat. As postwar standards of living rose, refrigeration became more widespread, and Americans came to expect fresh meat more often. In turn, meat was marketed more and more aggressively. Americans ate 140 pounds of beef, pork, and lamb per capita in 1960; in 1997, total meat consumption amounted to 190 pounds per person. At around the same time, the commercial meat industry saw the rise of the feedlot and an explosion in the number of industrial meat-processing plants.

In response to the cruelty of factory farming, a war against the traditional factory-farmed meat industry that shot animals full of hormones, electrocuted them, and turned them into meat was waged from the 1970s onward. Joshua Harper is part of that war. He was a member of the group Stop Huntingdon Animal Cruelty

(SHAC), organizing against the Huntingdon Life Sciences laboratory in New Jersey. (He was also involved with West Coast animal defense groups and a similar organization in Arkansas.) The lab was famous for conducting animal testing for various businesses, mostly pharmaceutical companies. Members ran and contributed to a website about laboratory testing, which posted the home addresses of Huntingdon's corporate officers and other employees (found in public reports and the phone book), along with a disclaimer that the SHAC group only advocated legal protest and thus weren't attempting to incite violence in others, according to the *Toronto Star*.

In 2004, six of the activists and the SHAC organization itself were charged with conspiracy under the Animal Enterprise Protection Act (AEPA) for "causing physical disruption of an animal enterprise." All six of the SHAC 7 were convicted and sentenced to years in prison.

Harper had been found guilty of using SHAC's site to foment attacks on companies that did business with the lab, in the hopes of closing the lab down entirely. At thirty-eight years old, he had already served his term in a federal prison and was working at a vegan restaurant in Portland, Oregon, named Blossoming Lotus. He was still involved in animal rights activism, archiving old animal rights and environmental publications and sharing them for free online, helping organize a conference on animal liberation in Portland, speaking about activism for nonhumans. He even still occasionally attended demonstrations.

Like David Lee, Harper had his epiphany after viewing animal suffering firsthand, when he first spotted poison pellets and then saw a nearby deer mouse dying. He still recalled with agitation the mouse that had "died on account of her species—she wanted to live and she wanted freedom. I knew I couldn't just talk about it, had to go out and fight."

Harper hadn't taken the road Lee and many of the other outsiders who were happy to get carnivores to buy into their politics did. Instead, he sacrificed years of his own life for his cause. He viewed liberating animals as part of a broader movement to release people, along with animals, from corporate dominance—represented by the pharmaceutical industry he had targeted—and from the inhumanity of such a system.

Harper's singular rage at animal abuse and animal death also stemmed, in part, from witnessing human brutality toward other humans. He told me he had had a violent father and drew parallels between the suffering of animal quarry and his own childhood *as* quarry. I sympathized to a degree; I had become a vegetarian at fourteen after identifying with the meat on the family table and crying over the devoured and killed bunnies in the film *Watership Down*. For twenty-five years I went through elaborate rigmarole so I could get soy milk in my coffee and avoid chicken in my salad. After speaking to the purist animal rights outsiders and reading their books, I realized I was like them. I, too, saw myself in creatures that had been exterminated and consumed. The sense that I also was an animal was what had prevented me from eating other animals.

But the position of purity and hyperidentification that Wise and Harper hold is something of a throwback, a remnant of the animal rights movement's edgy, preassimilated identity, before it was packaged into animal-testing-free shampoo or YouTube videos. What could the future of such a movement hold if it wished to be effective? Will its assimilated side and its purists ever come to be synthesized? Then I came upon a third group that combines the Animal Rights Lite crowd and, to some extent, the purists, but with a technological ideal. Their dream? Real steaks eaten with no animals harmed.

ANIMAL RIGHTS FUTURISTS

The final stage of the renegadeism around meat isn't necessarily what you might expect. When I first heard about those I consider to be animal rights futurists, they seemed like something out of the film *Soylent Green* or perhaps *Frankenstein*—and, in a way, they sort of were.

Vladimir Mironov is a scientist focused on creating cultured meat, a "meat" produced in a lab from animal cells, not from a real live creature, in a process in which no more than one animal is harmed. It's about as far from earthy nature as you can get, yet it could be the very solution to the problem of killing for meat that so many animal rights activists and vegetarians seek.

It's true that you initially need a few muscle cells from a cow. Hypothetically, tons of meat could then be grown and harvested using that cow's cells. The process requires animal muscle cells called myoblasts, which must be taken directly from an animal, which is why at least one must die. Magnified, myoblasts resemble caviar. When they fuse together, they create skeletal muscle fibers, the kind we use to walk and to exercise. Out of these fibers, ultimately, meat could be created. If the cells are grown in the proper medium using the necessary technology, which involves a five-story bioreactor, they could make enough meat to feed America, Mironov says.

With Jason Gaverick Matheny, Mironov co-founded New Harvest, a group that promotes work on artificial meat (one of the *New York Times Magazine*'s ideas of the year for 2005). Mironov and fellow scientists are using new technologies in order to give humans the food they desire without harming huge numbers of animals. If cultured meat is ever made in large enough quantities to meet the market demands of millions of people, it will constitute the biggest step forward ever for animal protection advocates. For those who want to eat animal flesh, cultured meat promises them a satisfying meal that is not made from a creature with a mind or a life. These activists' and scientists' great, elusive hope is that animals will no longer die on factory farms.

The idea was that if you bit into a burger made of artificial meat, you might not even notice the difference between its taste and texture and that of a grilled hamburger made from beef. PETA had offered a $1 million prize to any scientist or engineer who could produce commercially viable quantities of artificial meat grown in a lab from animal cells. As Bruce Friedrich, formerly vice president of policy for PETA and now senior director for strategic initiatives at Farm Sanctuary, put it to me, "Growing a corpse in a lab, to me, is less aesthetically revolting than eating a corpse of an animal that once lived. That animal had been mired in misery at a farm and then slaughtered in unhappy adolescence." (The prize is somewhat ironic, since some food scientists regard PETA and its ilk as lab-hating enemies: PETA was sued by the Huntingdon Life Sciences lab after PETA sent in an undercover worker and then publicly released the results.) The contest's catch: the winner must be able to make enough artificial meat to market the product in at least ten U.S. states at a competitive price.

In 2012, outside of San Francisco, Patrick Brown, a vegan professor at Stanford University, was also trying to cook up both artificial meat and dairy products in a lab. Like Mironov, his main goal was to "make a food for people who are comfortable eating meat and who want to continue eating meat. I want to reduce the human footprint on this planet by 50%," he told the *Guardian*. Unlike Mironov, he was trying to use plant material to create simulated meat, rather than drawing on animal cells.

Mironov worked alone. Born in a small town near Moscow, he conformed to the cliché of the Russian scientist: when I met with him in 2008, he was a fifty-five-year-old chain-smoker, a tall, bearish man with a loud laugh, a warmly nihilistic demeanor, and tobacco-stained teeth surrounded by a small gray beard. At his lab at the Basic Sciences Building at the University of South Carolina in Charleston, Mironov showed me a paper on which he had drawn animal muscle cells, a bioreactor that can turn these cells into meat, and a hamburger with arrows running between them. While we talked, he got a message on his answering machine about five fetal porcine hearts he needed for his experiments. Such is his life.

Mironov's preferred neologism for cultured meat was *Charlam*, "Charleston artificial meat." He said the name gives the would-be meat what he called "the charm and dignity" that is its due. (A scientist can dream.)

What if real meat didn't come from an animal? It's a radical notion. For him, the ambition to create it springs from a desire to solve a scientific problem and participate in a revolution rather than from an ethical principle. He had carnivorous eating habits to rival those of any red-blooded Russian; when we met, he boasted of the quality of the cut of beef he had eaten the previous night. But for those eagerly awaiting cultivated meat—who imagine we might split the difference between consumer pleasure and consumer guilt—affordable Charlam is a possible answer.

Making artificial meat isn't cheap; to make the cells blossom into savory burgers would cost millions. As Mironov put it, "The artificial meat hamburger is more expensive than gold, $5,000 or so." Others have estimated that it may cost as much as $250,000 to develop a single burger, at least until it can be mass-produced. And there are significant taste challenges, for flesh is a complex mesh of muscle and gristle whose distinct flavor and texture have proved hard to fake.

At Eindhoven University of Technology in the Netherlands, tissue engineers supported by the Dutch government have already designed bioreactors that can make small-animal muscle tissue grow swiftly, but all agree that we are just at the beginning. Mironov, for one, wasn't sure he would see mass-produced, widely available, affordable artificial meat in his lifetime due to lack of funding, although a Dutch artificial meat scientist has put the time frame closer to ten years. Before it reaches the mass market, Mironov suggested that Charlam might first be sold at a "food bar for Hollywood." An exclusive bar could offer a mixture of artificial meat, nuts, and perhaps kinesin, a protein that he said was a weight-reducing ingredient found in cockroaches and shellfish. He imagined film stars of the future taking a special liking to it.

When I checked in on him in 2012, his lab at the University of South Carolina had been shut down and his project had been suspended indefinitely, due to a confidential dispute with colleagues. He was working in Brazil. His "cultured meat" project had been transferred to the University of Missouri at Columbia, where a PETA-funded researcher, Nicholas Genovese, now presided.

Eating artificial meat doesn't necessarily mean that we see

ourselves as animals, however. This is where the animal rights futurists and animal rights purists cleave. The purists use the phrases *human animals* and *nonhuman animals*, underlining the similarities rather than differences between animals and humans, stressing closeness and reciprocity. We must see animals *as* us, they say. The most truly radical challenge of animal rights is getting people to see that they are not substantively different from animals.

Wise and others like him are trying to break down the line between humans and animals. Intellectual luminaries in other disciplines concur. The philosopher Giorgio Agamben's work attempts to conjoin humans and animals, using the status and abuses of animals as a way of thinking about human rights and about how we privilege them over animal rights. True human rights, it would seem, would also require animal rights as well. Theorist Donna Haraway, an emeritus professor at the University of California at Santa Cruz, distrusts the boundaries between animals and humans and is the author of such books as *Simians, Cyborgs and Women: The Reinvention of Nature* and *The Companion Species Manifesto: Dogs, People, and Significant Otherness.*

These scholars offer the most high-minded, incorporeal ways of getting "beyond meat." But there have been plenty of bottom-line, material victories, both for the animal rights purists and for the Animal Rights Lite types. In 2008, the state of California voted in favor of Proposition 2, which prevented housing chickens in tiny cages; their pens are legally required to be the chicken equivalent of Motel 6 rooms rather than New York City subway cars at rush hour. It also prevented the use of veal crates for calves and gestation crates for breeding pigs.

The ballot initiative passed by a huge margin, 63 percent to 37 percent, and will ultimately alter the way twenty million hens will live out their chickeny lives. It is considered to be one of the biggest animal protection initiatives ever in America. (A lighter California law, which went into effect in 2012, banned the delicacy foie gras, which requires the mass force-feeding of birds to enlarge their livers and was once the hallmark of a classy gathering.)

Yet purists such as Wise don't think their work is anywhere near done or can be bundled into products or propositions. While the animal rights movement has increasingly become the stuff of celebrity campaigns and Whole Foods—and thus one of the clearest case studies of the fringes drifting toward the center of America—Wise still sees animal rights as a moral issue that few human beings have taken to heart. Some of his camera-ready animal rights colleagues disagree with his purist approach. They are the ones infiltrating the mainstream with the hope that change can happen one vegan sausage—or vegetarian video—at a time.

7

BEYOND MASS MARKETS

In one tent, I watched 3-D printers create three-dimensional objects out of thin air. In another tent, a child showed off his hand-built robots. Outside on a fairground, a jerry-built scooter raised a man high above the crowd as it skidded past a woman with purple yarn knitted into her cornrows. Giant bicycles for two with butterfly wings attached to them rolled past me. I stopped in a booth and was offered earrings and necklaces made of industrial rubber carved so finely they appeared to be made of ivory. At another booth, I could buy entirely natural lipsticks made by a chemist who offered to concoct a custom reddish brown shade for me that would match my skin.

It was the yearly Maker Faire, which was held in Queens, New York, in 2012, a craft fair extravaganza of amateurs and artisans showing and selling a torrent of handmade products and technological experiments. This is where I met bead-and-flower jewelry maker Jenine Bressner, years after I first saw her blown glass necklaces, which looked like tropical fish crossed with paramecia on a lab slide.

Bressner told everyone who would listen that she was trying to combine "technology and the future" with "old-fashioned craft." She pointed to more than a dozen neon-colored cloth flowers that she had laser-cut and hung around her booth. The flowers also encircled a metal halo attached to her head. In addition, Bressner wore a giant glass bead necklace around her neck; she had blown each of the beads herself. The whole thing looked like a Day-Glo hallucination.

"I don't want to perpetuate a disposable culture," Bressner told me, handing me a fuchsia bracelet composed of her fabric flowers. She hated the "shoddily made and mass-produced." She believed that when people purchased a T-shirt, they should know not only what they were buying but whom they were buying from. As she started one of her spiels, her mom smiled at me knowingly. The sticker "Mom of a Maker" was affixed to her lapel. I found out she still worked, as she has for the past forty years, at a blood bank.

Bressner was thirty-four years old. When she wasn't at craft fairs, she lived in a Providence, Rhode Island, warehouse whose interior she had built herself. Even her bed and her shoes were handmade; almost every prefabricated thing in her place she had Dumpster-dived for.

"I want to know how to do everything for myself," Bressner said. "I believe everyone can do everything for themselves. So much of the stuff out there is gross and crappy. I am here to show people how to make better stuff for themselves. It's what my life is about." She spends eight hours a day making glass beads. She also creates and streams free Web tutorials to help people make similar objects using downloadable kits.

Bressner is just one of many crafters highly—even painfully—attuned to what they see as the corruption wrought by industrial manufacturing. Some of the makers who attend Maker

Faires are enamored with both the past and the present; they download dress patterns and then sew their own clothes. They worship the bespoke, the homemade, "the natural," and the pre-industrial; they are a chorus saying that not everything needs to be commoditized on a grand scale and that we can grow or make anything that is typically produced in an industrial fashion, from wallets to beer. They are nouveau Shakers in a world of mass-market franchising. What they produce is not always terribly radical on the face of it—it can often be endearingly bumpy and half-cocked instead. Such makers create hooked rugs depicting foxy women undressed and writhing, soda caps with tiny illustrations of mice or giraffes that resemble the interiors of Joseph Cornell boxes, steampunk cufflinks made of hundred-year-old windup-watch parts, and coasters and bowls made from old LPs.

These crafters are not sharp-edged outsiders or mind-bending rebels or disturbing renegades. Rather, they exist on the lighter side of the continuum; they are the people midcentury sociologist Erving Goffman called the "quietly disaffiliated," people whose hobbies and passionate activities take them a little out of conventional society, but not entirely. The makers can also be considered another example of "pro-ams," or professional amateurs, a group identified in Charles Leadbeater and Paul Miller's 2004 essay "The Pro-Am Revolution: How Enthusiasts Are Changing Our Economy and Society." This new breed pursues amateur activities to high standards and has redefined their leisure not as passive consumerism but as active participation: pursuing something such as bargello or clockmaking to "professional standards" is one way to simultaneously exceed and negotiate with the knowledge elite in any given area. Many of the people in this book are pro-ams, and the pro part of them means they are better equipped to work with and impress financial gatekeepers, professional interpreters, and regulators than the usual outsider or nonprofessional.

The Church of Craft was a prime example of pro-am. Founded in 2000 in Brooklyn, by 2011 it had thirteen chapters around the country that met monthly to make knitwear or sew. Its mostly female congregations embraced even the most esoteric crafting pursuits—there was even a maker of bobbin lace. At the Church of Craft, communal purling was considered a spiritual activity, and every product made or purchased in this handmade way led, it seemed, to the crafter or buyer donning a macramé halo. Like any church, it provided its members with a belief system and an ethical framework that insists on things being grown and bought and sold locally, in a fashion that could be sustained over the long term.

Callie Janoff is the Church of Craft's founder, forty-three years old and a graduate of the Union Theological Seminary. She began the church to "serve as the physical community" for crafters' many virtual ones. "I think of craft as something timeless," she said. "There's always been a subversive quality to hand making— a lot of antislavery quilts, for instance."

In the 1990s, thousands, and then hundreds of thousands, of people began to create and sell handmade, amateur goods with a newfound earnestness. These people were crafters—knitters, seamstresses, woodworkers—who called themselves "makers." It was no surprise that these alternative crafters started renovating their identities with needlepoint during a recession: crafting tends to flourish in times of economic downturn. Here were hard-core believers in the transformative power of making your own stuff, selling your own stuff, and buying stuff directly from the people who had made it. Crafters formed groups with such colorful names as Petal to the Metal, the Glitter Workshop, Knitta, and the Felt Club. By 2008, a Maker Faire (the first of which was held in 2006 in San Mateo, California) drew 65,000 people to Austin, Texas.

After the movement was off and running, the sustainability of the materials used became even more of a primary consideration. Makers started to wonder: what if millions of pounds of the 13.1 million tons of textiles that were discarded in 2010 could be recycled? That's 5 percent of the municipal solid waste in the United States. In 2010, only an estimated 15 percent of those textiles were recovered for recycling. What if almost all of them could be reclaimed? What if a buyer could rest assured nothing she bought was made in a sweatshop? Dissatisfied with the ways most people ate and shopped, while underemployed during a recession, these renegades tried to return to what they believed was an older, better way to live.

Janoff, for example, wanted only hand-stitched objects in her life. "I am not going to buy anything but handmade clothes," she told me. As she wrote on her site, "Our consumption plagues our quiet lives, filling it with broadcast noise and boxes of macaroni and cheese. But when we make something, we are filled with satisfaction, the kind you feel to your core." After working five to ten hours a week as a freelance bookkeeper, she would rush home to craft or to attend craft meetings, always trying to get there "before the start time to work on whatever project." At Church of Craft meetings, she greeted other crafters one by one as they drifted in. One might be in her early sixties, one in her late fifties, another a young single mother, and the fourth a college student.

At a typical meeting, Janoff was surrounded by people cutting a skirt, embroidering, crocheting, and making lace (actually, something called tatting, where you handcraft lace using knots and loops). Janoff herself mostly makes socks because, she said, they are healing and portable.

"Crafting is a lot of work to make a living," Janoff said. "It can be done in a subversive vein: I can make this, so I *will* make this. I live in the island of Manhattan now, which is one giant mall, and it's hard to avoid Starbucks. So I try to create my own world. I make my brown-bag lunch, and when my old underwear fails, I am going to avoid the Gap and buy them on Etsy, where they'll cost a little more, but the designer will make them to my measurements."

Another Church of Craft member, Reine Hewitt, who lives in Tarrytown, New York, knits and sells blankets and crochets women's necklaces—even an organic red snake made of yarn. Her blankets take a year to make. She uses cotton and soy silk and made most of her own baby's bibs. She likes to "keep stuff on the needles," as she put it. "If I am not making stuff, something is wrong," she said. "It's how I stay stable in the world." She goes to the Church of Craft meetings because it "offers some kind of peace and comfort." (Her ideal is to become a reverend in the church, like Janoff, who delivers short "sermon" videos about the power of craft that can be seen on the Church of Craft site.)

All of these crafters exposed themselves to an ever-present tension: they defined themselves by what they consumed even as they positioned themselves in opposition to an increasingly disposable consumer culture. They also had to heavily sell themselves and their products in order to survive in an increasingly competitive marketplace. When they weren't happy about these self-definitions, they tried to finesse them by creating a consumer and producer identity that aimed to be neither shallow nor entirely revolutionary. They made clothes or clocks made from recycled cloth or parts.

CRAFT INCORPORATED

Crafters often rely on the concept of authenticity, although it is a notion long ago disputed and absorbed by advertising. Today's craft culture is appropriated by or shares the stage with the very homogenous branded gear made by faraway machines that it purportedly opposes. At the Maker Faire, for instance, mixed in with the makers were booths for major conglomerates, from Schick "eco" razors to Zipcar. The alternative craft scene has been appropriated, at least as a metaphor, by chain stores such as Urban Outfitters taking the individualized DIY aesthetic, mass-producing clothes with ragged hems or machine-made approximations of hand stitching. The Urban Outfitters blog is full of helpful and giggle-worthy uses of craftivism (the combination of craft and activism), linking to sites where you can buy porcupine quill jewelry or turn old sinks into planters.

The most complicated instance of this—at once an example of crafters' power and their vulnerability to big companies— is the craft site Etsy. Etsy was founded in June 2005; by 2012, 800,000 active sellers were hawking their wares on the site. Most of Etsy's members subscribe to the mantra "Mass production is over." At last count, the site hosted 17 million listed items and enjoyed 1.4 billion monthly page views. It grossed $525.6 million in sales in 2011. By selling to individual buyers around the world,

Etsy ran not on advertising revenue but rather on the aggregated proceeds of individuals buying from other individuals. (The profits the company makes from the transactions, at 20 cents per item, are modest but add up.) The vast majority of sellers are hobbyists and other nonprofessionals.

Etsy's affable young communications guy Adam Brown, who makes costumes by hand and had built his own house, told me the company aimed to offer an "alternative to mass production— knowing who you are buying from and knowing how they made their stuff." As he spoke, he got glitter on his elbows from sitting at one of the office's "craft stations." The company ran on the basic faith that if we have the option to buy cups and bowls directly from a DIY crafter, we will, rather than from Walmart or Crate and Barrel, even if they cost less at those chain stores. Within this belief system, supporting a local seller (being a shopavore) is ethical and authentic. Knowing that a specific person made the object you bought—someone who did it because that's what he or she wanted to do—is always worth the higher price. In the *Atlantic*, the writer Sara Horowitz described Etsy as part of a "sharing economy . . . based on people coming together to create their own markets." This "sharing" economy, which in Horowitz's telling included Zipcar and Kickstarter, was creating "a quiet revolution."

The makers I spoke to didn't talk about Etsy with transformational fervor, although I guessed that, deep down, they probably were hoping that sharing and selling shawls and handmade clocks as part of a larger community would in fact prove somehow revolutionary. "The craft-selling thing became more serious when Etsy came about and provided a platform for a microeconomy," Janoff told me. Before that, "you would be working three or four times as hard" to create a craft website and to market that site, she said; you had to rely on listservs, eBay, and a hodgepodge of sites and craft fairs.

Etsy and the millions attracted to the site proved to be the mainstreaming of a model for a different kind of shopping. In 2007, Etsy's founders pledged: "The connection between producer and consumer has been lost. We created Etsy to help them reconnect, and swing the pendulum back to a time when we bought our bread from the baker, food from the grocer, and shoes from the cobbler. Our vision is to build a new economy and present a better choice: Buy, Sell, and Live Handmade." Etsy's "craftivism" team declared that by "buying and selling directly from the maker, we are challenging the all-pervasive corporate culture that promotes profit over people" and celebrating those who "spin yarn, sew, hammer, forge, glue, knit, knot, alter and sculpt with an eye towards creating new forms of commerce and the making of goods."

At the Etsy headquarters, located on a giant floor of a loft building in Brooklyn, room after room was decorated with the handmade products of Etsy sellers: a chair made from a stuffed bear, an owl-shaped lamp, "felt-a-dermy" animal-free taxidermy heads (e.g., a crafted replica of a stuffed moose head made of fabric and glued to a backboard). Employees attached "I Heart Homemade" bumper stickers to their computers as if they were découpage shingles. One room featured a wall of kitschy 1980s album covers. (Etsy permitted the sale of only certain non-handmade items, which had to be "vintage"—that is, at least twenty years old.) I spotted an octopus made of socks: a socktopus.

Etsy goes out of its way to celebrate the tenderly homey, objects whose bruised quirkiness is intended to warm the heart, both by filling every corner of the huge office space with them and by keeping a craft room open to the public for "making events." Going beyond traditional sales has been remarkably profitable for the company. In 2010, the site had an estimated value of $300 million and projected revenues of approximately $30 million to $50 million. By 2012, the company had three-hundred-plus employees and stated it had sold $65 million worth of goods in just one month of that year. The wealth has spread to at least some of the makers out there, and a few hundred of the site's "featured sellers" have been able to quit their day jobs, according to the company. (Nevertheless, in 2009, Sara Mosle, writing in *Slate*'s "XX Factor" section, questioned how common financial success on Etsy really is in an article titled "Etsy.com Peddles a False Feminist Fantasy," writing, "There's little evidence that most sellers on the site make much money.")

"Etsy is another manifestation of how D.I.Y.-ism has evolved," Rob Walker wrote in the *New York Times Magazine* in 2007. While it may still be imagined to be a way to help hipsters free themselves from capitalism, Etsy is really, at best, closer to "independence *within* capitalism." If anything, the evolution of DIY brings it back to common capitalist pursuits.

Julie Schneider worked for Etsy. She also both made goods from recycled materials—she sometimes even made her own shoes—and bought her basic goods on Etsy. She saw it as a small way of "rethinking how the economy works. I go to craft fairs because I like to meet the person who made the print and hear the story behind the print." She explained, "It has more meaning than the anonymous big box retail store: I want to hear about the makers' backgrounds, how they came to make what they are making. I always want to hear it in the first person, so it's a personal marketplace."

In the middle of the nineteenth century, the Etsy equivalent was charity bazaars, where women who were barred from mainstream buying and selling could participate in the craft fairs of their day. In the world at large, these women had to struggle to represent their own financial interests, but in the space of the charity bazaar they could negotiate with sellers directly, with prices fluctuating during a single day; best of all, they could wind up selling something they had made themselves. The bazaar retained older forms of market transaction: the seller was face-to-face with the buyer, and a lot of sales success rested on how much both parties liked each other. Even then, the idea was that these gewgaws were things you couldn't get in any ordinary store.

Craft took off starting in the 1840s: everyone was told to do it, said Talia Schaffer, a professor of English at the City University of New York Graduate Center and the author of *Novel Craft: Victorian Domestic Handicraft and Nineteenth-Century Fiction*. She explained that there were two variations on craft even then: one school of craft insisted objects be unique, well-constructed, and made of good materials, in contrast to the mass-produced objects that were suddenly flooding the marketplace. The other held that craft meant that everyday people could and should create whatever they wished, like using ready-made kits.

Schaffer said, "The *Good Housekeeping* traditional craft continues"—referring to the ready-made, less "creative" craft, which emphasizes good execution—"and it's different from the cool Etsy way of doing it," which emphasizes personal expression and purported originality.

The Arts and Crafts movement, which started in England in the mid-nineteenth century and then migrated to the United States, championed the making and selling of wood furniture and other useful objects separate from factories' mass production and impersonal sales. At the time, manufactured goods and consumption were on the rise, and the Arts and Crafters argued that if individual craftsmanship could be brought back, a different, more authentic relationship would arise between human beings and the manufactured goods around them—they would be, in the words of William Morris, one of the sages of the movement, "for the people and by the people, and a source of pleasure to the maker and the user." Neither workers nor consumers would be degraded by impersonal, inhumane business exchanges; instead, both groups would be more personally invested with the products they made or used. In his book *No Place of Grace: Antimodernism and the Transformation of American Culture, 1880–1920*, T.J. Jackson Lears described the Arts and Crafts movement as people attempting "antimodern dissent" through chairs and wood. The woodworkers and the like were flouting technology and urban luxury while seeking to rejuvenate what they considered the "overcivilized personality" of Americans.

Today's makers and Etsyans are a different beast, of course, in part because technological developments didn't necessarily repel them. People such as Bressner used technology heavily in their homespun efforts. In addition, the omnipresence of the virtual world may be leading the makers—and the rest of us—to crave the real, the tactile, and the concrete all the more, whether we yearn for the dirt that gives rise to organic vegetables or the wool we plan to spin ourselves. Perhaps omnipresent technology demands a dose of the antimodern and the Luddite?

"When there's stress and change in the mainstream economy, like at the heyday of industrialism," Schaffer explained, things such as craft and farming tend to reemerge. Crafters will take the "signature economic development of their period that they feel like they are excluded from and turn that exclusion into a virtue." She points to my iPhone case, which was designed to look like a tape cassette. "It's like, we crafters can make mass-produced-looking things by hand. Just because I am sitting at home doesn't mean that I can't churn out products."

Gargantuan impersonal stores, selling products shipped from thousands of miles away, fill our cities and towns, and in response we feel a growing need to exercise some control over what we buy and sell. Is it possible to avoid Walgreens, Amazon, and Whole Foods, as the urban farmers and crafters urge, and try to shop around them?

At the Maker Faire in September 2012, I saw "improvisatory" sewers who offered to make shirts, hats, and bags in less than two hours; MacGyver-esque inventions, such as a homemade rocket; and a musician playing an electric guitar that had been rigged as a conduit for eight different instruments (the musical style is called Controllerism—who knew?). In the past, Americans did projects like this alone in their garages and rec rooms and kept the results to themselves. Now they go online to brag every time their homemade Tesla coil manages to give off a spark.

When these makers ask us to buy their stuff, it is not just an apolitical lark. It also can be seen as an increasingly necessary antidote to shopping at franchise stores like Urban Outfitters, whose conservative co-founder and CEO Richard Hayne gave money to political candidates who opposed gay marriage (including $30,000 to Mitt Romney) and may well funnel money to other causes not all of the chain's shoppers support. At the Maker Faire, every sale was conducted by people hand-selling work they had made themselves. Their profits wouldn't filter up to a multinational company whose political ties even a hyper-vigilant observer of corporate transgressions couldn't begin to track.

GROWING IT

In one corner of Brooklyn, hens and rabbits ran around their cages. Kale grew in neat rows next to nasturtiums, baby lettuce, and daisies. Some members of a swarm of twenty thousand bees buzzed in circles near their beehives in the midday heat. One farmer watered vegetables, while another gathered freshly picked kale to deliver to a local pizzeria that would use it to adorn vegetarian pies. Other farmers and volunteers sorted through eggs from the chickens and gathered herbs from the farm to make herb butter that they would sell on Sunday on their roof. They would pick and wash radishes and their leaves, which they would also sell. Every weekend, one of the farmers would give a lecture, whether on composting, soap making, or foraging for edible weeds.

I had taken three different subways to get to this farm. I walked to a bleak block where a sign pleading "Do Not Litter" stood guard over a heap of rubbish. The smell was pure: pure gasoline. I then walked up a flight of dingy stairs to reach a fire escape. When I climbed up and finally stood among the farm's dirt rows, I was on an urban roof. Nearby I could see a giant crane, with dozens more of them lying on their sides—a crane farm. A big industrial ship idled on the bank of the East River.

This was Eagle Street Rooftop Farm, a six-thousand-square-foot rooftop farm that was co-founded by twenty-eight-year-old Annie Novak in 2009, underwritten by the building's owner, Broadway Stages, a film company that rented out its giant interiors as film and television sets. Broadway Stages was interested in urban agriculture as a form of environmental activism, in part because the movie industry is a known big polluter. They weren't alone, as Long Island City's Silvercup Studios, where *Sex and the City* was filmed, housed one of New York City's largest green roofs. Eagle Street Rooftop Farm was built by Chris Goode, an architect who has created several green rooftops in New York City. Ben Flanner was Novak's collaborator. (Flanner later left Eagle Street to found the Brooklyn Grange, another rooftop farm that, despite the name, is in another borough, Queens.) The entire staff was in their twenties and almost wholly female, except for the occasional very genial male volunteer. Novak and a few others were paid, but most worked for free. (In their off time, farm workers might find themselves battling their landlords for the right to grow vegetables in an unused garage, as Alice Forbes Spear did.)

Some staffers said they were trying to circumvent supermarkets and the FreshDirect grocery delivery service by consuming things they grew themselves, relying on small-scale consumer culture both to make money—they sold their produce to at least nine restaurants—and to invest their labor with meaning. They felt that the kind of commerce they engaged in was not just a business but also an ethos.

Urban farmers, like crafters, often seek to escape the world of the mass-produced. The farmers at Eagle Street and at Brooklyn Grange decided to green their city rather than escape and seek respite in natural enclaves outside New York. Their choice helps puncture the old-fashioned idea of nature as existing only in the wilderness and as something necessarily pure. Instead, urban farmers reclaim cities as part of nature, making them greener and more environmentally sound by refurbishing empty lots. Such work goes on in ravaged cities such as Detroit and Rust Belt cities including Cleveland, as well as in New York City. These urban green farmers refuse to abandon decaying cities for a pastoral dream or to scorn wealthier urban spaces as too ripe with money and gentrification. As writer Rebecca Solnit wrote in the magazine *Orion*, "Sales of vegetable seeds have skyrocketed across the country. Backyard chickens have become a new norm, and schoolyard gardens have sprung up across the nation."

In the past ten years, local governments in Chicago and New York have passed measures to encourage tree planting and awarded substantial tax abatements to urban farms that use rainwater, as well as giving incentives to builders or companies that create roofs full of flowers and foliage; such green roofs can help heat and cool buildings without using electricity or gas and reduce air pollution. Eagle Street remains tax-exempt, and in 2008, New York offered one-year tax abatements for new buildings with grassy tops. By 2010, Cleveland had become home to about 1,200 urban gardens.

Like crafters, urban farmers are trying to break down the borders between making and consuming, even between work and fun. The farmers also see their work as a potential alternative to industrial agriculture, as well as a cure for food shortages. It constitutes a strand of the environmental movement that seeks out nature in the man-made, unnatural world of the city. Urban environmentalists such as writer and scholar Jenny Price try to expose "the wilderness" as a construct whose time has passed. "To define nature as the wild things apart from cities is one of the great fantastic American stories," she wrote in the essay "Thirteen Ways of Seeing Nature in L.A." "And it's one of the great fantastic American denials . . . *Is there nature in L.A.?* Far more than our philosophies dream of, and much more than in Portland or Boulder—more, possibly, on Mapleton Drive alone than in some small towns in Iowa." Environmental historian William Cronon also criticizes what he feels to be outdated escapist attitudes toward the natural world in *Uncommon Ground: Rethinking the Human Place in Nature*, a book he edited.

Others saw even more complicated ideas embedded in the countercultural farmers. Some made a point of calling themselves "urban agriculturalists," with the stress on *urban*, the famed New Urbanist architect Andres Duany told me. They reinforced his theory of urban areas: there should be smaller, denser clusters of homes and walkable paths, all surrounded by edible gardens, re-creating cities so that they would resemble traditional communities before the car.

AGRICULTURATI

I could see how farms such as Brooklyn's Eagle Street might be dismissed as trendy or self-indulgent, part of a hipster obsession with pleasing your taste buds that allowed young people to divert all "real" politics into perfect homegrown amaranth, spaghetti squash, or aged raspberry vinegar. When I visited on a market day, it seemed to deserve some of that pigeonholing. The radish leaf pesto was pricey, although I appreciated its classy generic label. The farm was a fine example of the locavore, but I realized that the range of associations with the overall movement was often not as legit. Foster Farms, a $1 billion poultry company, marketed its fresh chicken and turkey as "locally grown" because it has contracts with local growers on the West Coast. In 2009, Frito-Lay made the case for its chips being locavore-ish, with ads in which a farmer in Florida noted that the chips were made in Florida.

This is all partly a result of urban farmers tracking mud into popular culture, with the requisite reality television shows, big book deals, and ubiquity on YouTube. The meme has been planted far and wide. Former pro basketball player Will Allen extolled his Milwaukee urban farm, Growing Power, in the press. Urban farmers meticulously blogged about city life with three chickens. Farmers with an online presence told anyone who would read them—and some reached audiences of thousands—the right time to plant rhubarb. Novella Carpenter, a farmer and blogger who built a farm on a street in Oakland, California, wrote a book about it, *Farm City*, that became a bestseller. Its first sentence declared that her farm was in a "ghetto." In celebrating the 1970s back-to-the-land backdrop of the urban farm movement that her parents were part of, Carpenter was trying to integrate the past and present and to have it "both ways": a backyard self-sufficiency of her own, combined with the bars, museums, and convenience stores of a city.

Carpenter and others embodied a belief in fresh produce. Without backyard space and good soil for all, the urban farm wasn't so fey. Yet at times urban farming could rest on the edge of food fetishism, where consumerist obsessions with the freshest, rarest, most unique produce means that vegetables must be sold moments after they were picked and only by people you personally know. In certain food-centered circles, it can seem as if all well-being derives from the seasonality of the radishes in your salad. Solnit wrote in *Orion* that while some farms are focused on political and emotional engagement, "other gardens and food fetishism generally can be a retreat into privilege, safety, and pleasure away from the world and its problems."

Yet some rooftop gardens and farm lots grow in the midst of the country's biggest problems. Take the farms of Detroit, for instance.

A LOT OF THEIR OWN

For fifteen years, Greg Willerer, now forty-three, was a public school teacher at a school in Detroit. He lived in Corktown, the city's oldest neighborhood. During the 2000s, Corktown started sliding down. Once a teeming area of residential homes and Irish immigrants, now some of its buildings, like the grand Michigan Central Station, are abandoned. The sidewalks have eroded, and most inhabitants walk in the middle of the street.

When Willerer looked at Detroit as a whole, he saw between thirty and forty square miles of vacant land and buildings within city limits. Part of the problem, of course, was housing foreclosures; according to RealtyTrac, the city saw 31,775 completed foreclosures in 2011. Like many industrial American cities, Detroit has been radically depopulated, its population falling by 25 percent in the first decade of the twenty-first century. As of 2011 it had just 706,000 inhabitants. While scanning this vacant horizon, Willerer had a revelation. He decided he would become a farmer—but not as an exodus from the city he loved and worked in. He would become a farmer *in* Detroit. He saw no reason to go "back to the land," as previous generations of Americans who had moved to, say, Vermont had done in order to create their own naturalist homesteads. So Willerer located and purchased an abandoned lot that was pretty much rubble with dead trees standing in it. Then he and other local residents got together, knocked down a lot of the trees, and carted them away. Once the area was cleared, the question remained: how could he convert this lot back into the farmland it once was? It would take more than just compost.

In Detroit, the city administration was less involved with promoting urban farming than other cities had been; instead, the movement was driven by residents working on their own or through a couple of organizations to green the city. At last count, Willerer's farm was one of thirty-seven in Detroit. Like a number of blighted cities that had been abandoned by heavy industry, the town was now growing new pockets of green.

From the beginning, Willerer knew he faced a formidable challenge: how would he make the farm work financially while remaining part of the neighborhood in which the farm was located and serving its people? He decided that, first, he would have to get his produce to the city's finest restaurants, which serve the remnant of a moneyed public in the city's suburbs. Then he could provide food for his less than well-off neighbors—who, because so many grocery stores in the inner city had shut down, often had only gas stations and liquor stores at which to shop for groceries. Furthermore, he would provide his neighbors with this food for free. On a typical summer day at Willerer's farm, a volunteer farmer served her homemade mung bean cakes. People who lived near the farm—some of whom might never have eaten or even heard of a mung bean before— were lining up for them.

While Eagle Street's Novak told me she was "just a farmer" while hoisting bamboo tomato planters onto her skinny shoulders, Willerer was a little less modest and a little more militant. "We [in Detroit] don't believe in giving corporate America our money," he told me, while standing up to his neck in lettuce and spinach. Each week during the spring of 2009, his acre of land produced two hundred pounds of salad mix, including uncommon lettuces such as sorrel and mizuna. That summer, you could see his dozen vegetable beds and three greenhouses flourishing in the middle of a city depicted over and over again as decaying. He believed that the best exchanges of goods and services happen quasi-independently of a swollen free market. "Urban farmers want to take control back—of the food they eat, the way it is sold, and what stores sell it," he said. "We lose control every time we buy processed food."

Despite the inherent limitations of crafting and urban farming—their smallness of scale, the difficulty of accessing farmland in cities—most of the urban farmers held to a shared fundamental precept. They believed growing things in cities was rebellion from city life, from industrial agriculture, and even from traditional environmentalism.

Most subcultures form in response to a perceived conformity or monolith. Enthusiastic artisans making their own spirits or canning their own beets, can be read as part of an alternative tendency toward rejecting technology and modernity. They also are a rejection of so-called professional careers that entail sitting at a desk and staring at a computer for many hours a day (careers like my own). In our co-optation-friendly world, these outsiders aren't telling their flock not to shop. They tell them to shop, but in a better way—and to make things as well. The hope is that the rest of us will learn from them and pay attention to not just *what* but from *whom* and *why* we are buying.

POSTSCRIPT

One day early in the summer of 2012, two men in crisp business attire were talking about plastic debit cards at the Manhattan office of a financial services company that routinely partnered with huge conglomerates to produce prepaid cards, such as Visa or Green Dot. The men were interested in negotiating a deal to launch a debit card line, and they assured the company that they would have a cooperative bank to go along with the cards eventually.

Starting a new line of debit or prepaid cards was not extraordinary by any means. Banks such as Chase predictably do it, but so do reality TV stars and hip-hop magnates from Kim Kardashian to Russell Simmons, aligned with MasterCard or Visa. Finance guru Suze Orman has her own card line, too. Prepaid cards have turned into a major industry, and a very profitable one. While bank-issued debit cards associated with checking accounts are usually fee-free, the now-defunct Kardashian Kard incurred a fee of $9.95 upon purchase and then twelve monthly fees of $7.95 for a minimum of one year, which meant that just getting to *use* the card for a year cost more than $100. Orman's prepaid debit card is less expensive but still charges a $3 activation fee and a $3 monthly maintenance fee. People who use these cards tend to be poor and struggling economically—those living from paycheck to paycheck. They are called the unbanked and the underbanked.

The two men were not, however, financial or entertainment insiders trying to make a buck off this population. Despite their suits and their surroundings, they were outsiders: Occupy Wall Street activists who were part of the movement's alternative banking group, the Occupy Bank Working Group. They focused on creating an Occupy card and they would return again and again to the financial services company to discuss their future bank card's features. The card was designed to be most helpful to the underbanked: Anyone could get and use it and it would be the cheapest on the market. The card would address a significant problem faced by America's poor: bank-issued debit cards, unlike these fee-driven debit cards, are free, but you must already have a certain amount of money in order to open a bank account. In order to obtain a prepaid card, you need only the amount on the card itself plus the additional amount the manufacturer charges. The value of the Occupy bank card would lie in its direct competition with the many predatory prepaid bank cards already out there.

Like Occupy Wall Street and its working groups, the Occupy banking group aspired to have no hierarchies or what one might call horizontal leadership. The closest they came to a leader, facilitator, or even a figurehead was Carne Ross, an Englishman who proved a suave guest on *The Colbert Report* when invited to speak about the Occupy card. The author of the book *The Leaderless Revolution: How Ordinary People Will Take Power and*

Change Politics in the 21st Century, by day Ross runs the non-profit Independent Diplomat, which provides diplomacy advisory services to nonstates or people living in threatened territories, such as Saharawis. I had vaguely known him for years and had read his first book, *Independent Diplomat: Dispatches from an Unaccountable Elite*. I knew he was in his late forties and had once been a brilliant young diplomat at the United Nations. He left the post in June 2002 but remained at the UK Foreign Office until he resigned from the Foreign Office in 2004 after giving then-secret evidence during the first official inquiry into the Iraq War (the so-called Butler Inquiry). He went on to found Independent Diplomat that same year to address what he called a "diplomatic deficit" in a system that marginalized many groups that were not represented by states.

I met up with Ross and heard about the Occupy Bank Working Group almost a year into the Occupy movement. It was after the movement's full flowering at Zuccotti Park, but I had been told—and felt sure—that this sector of the Occupy movement was one to watch. For one thing, the underbanked made up a huge sector of the U.S. population. In 2011, one in twelve American households was unbanked, according to a Federal Deposit Insurance Corporation survey. Twenty percent of households were underbanked, meaning that while they had a bank account, they also relied on pawnshops, payday loans, and other means of off-label banking.

From a distance, Occupy as a whole seemed to be the apotheosis of the rise of the outsider: all of these amateurs, renegades, freaks, and idealists crowded together, altering the mainstream conversation. As one of the people behind the Occupy card put it to me, a strength of the movement—as with so many of the movements and creative efforts in this book—was an ability to change the broader language used by people outside the movement. Extend the "Occupy" analogy far enough, and it could mean something as basic as changing the way people worked, ate, or spent money. The broader Occupy movement clearly spoke to the power of amateurs and rebels. By the time I encountered the Occupy banking group, the movement had already helped make income inequality the crucial issue of the 2012 presidential elections and showed the effectiveness of ostensibly fringe and marginal positions to change the public conversation.

I had seen Ross around town at parties or talks, always in well-tailored suits, black hair slicked back, and sporting Elvis Costello glasses. His fashion sense was at odds with his extreme color blindness—he was, in fact, so color-blind that he couldn't become a fighter pilot, his first career choice, and had entered a diplomatic career instead. After the financial crisis hit, it took Ross a long time to understand its extent; he hadn't paid a lot of attention to Lehman Brothers' crash at the time. But then he started to read about finance, about how banks borrow money at a nominal amount and lend it to ordinary people at a higher rate, and about how bankers are forced by the market, he thought, to behave in certain destructive ways.

Banks are known to gamble assets. The resulting foreclosure crisis, in which millions of Americans lost their homes and couldn't pay their mortgages, was a case in point. After the collapse of the banks and the bailout in 2008, Ross no longer believed the government could actually regulate big banks. After all, bankers have extraordinary access to those in power, he noted. He said that the CEO of JPMorgan Chase, Jamie Dimon, "can see people at the White House. Who else can do that?" For him, the centralized authority of the banks was part of the problem, as such power was likely to foster corruption and selfish pursuits. As a feeling of powerless rage grew, he started to fantasize about flipping the banking relationship, so that users owned the bank rather than the other way around.

One hot evening in June of 2012, Ross, wearing his usual suit and tie, arrived late at an alternative banking meeting. The meeting was held at the large, dark loft apartment of one of the group's members, James Sherry, who had worked for IBM for decades and Morgan Stanley for over a year, while publishing experimental poetry in his spare time; he was now retired. Nearly everyone else in the room was a former or current Wall Street executive or had worked on the New York Stock Exchange; usually meetings were composed of 50 percent financial services workers, current or former. They were all middle-aged and as far from the mainstream Occupy stereotypes as could be imagined—no scruffy college students, beardy weirdies, or even full-time activists. Almost all of these people had "straight" jobs and had worked at them for many decades. They were bankers and looked the part. (In fact, some were so "inside" the system they were rebelling against that they insisted to journalists that they had to remain anonymous lest they lose their jobs.) The Occupy Bank Working Group had strengths: members were highly knowledgeable and highly specialized. They were able to use the technical language of financial services insiders while leveraging outsider identities, values, ideas, and goals.

The group had started meeting soon after the Occupy movement emerged in September 2011, with its first meeting in October. At the first meeting of what was then called the Alternative Banking Working Group, which was planned by

Ross, the group chose to split into smaller units. These consisted of the Occupy Bank Working Group, with which Ross was most involved; the Alternative Banking Working Group; and a third group that started independently, Occupy the SEC.

Both the Alternative Banking group and Occupy the SEC thought their goal should be to reform the current banking system as it is. Members sent polite, detailed letters to the U.S. Senate Committee on Banking, Housing, and Urban Affairs urging stronger regulation. In February 2012, members of Occupy the SEC, "concerned citizens, activists and financial professionals," sent a 325-page letter to financial regulators regarding what they saw as dangerous loopholes in the Volcker Rule; it must have been one of the most meticulous documents sent to the Securities and Exchange Commission in response to that legislation. One of the key members, Alexis Goldstein, had worked at Morgan Stanley, Deutsche Bank, and other financial firms. Many other members had similar résumés, and they were able to create such a substantial and critical close reading of the Volcker Rule thanks to their prior work experience in financial services. As a result of their letter, the group was invited to go to Washington and meet congressional staffers and SEC officials.

But Ross argued that the group's aim should be to set up new institutions, because citizens couldn't rely on the current system; tinkering with the regulations wouldn't do enough to help them. The Occupy Bank Working Group wanted to create its own bank and banking services, on the premise that the existing options were unredeemable.

Members batted back and forth the question of how to produce the card, with some in Montreal, Arizona, and elsewhere participating virtually. The scene couldn't have been more different from an evening at the Occupy encampment in Zuccotti Park months before or at the many Occupy sites in other cities. Here we were in a comfortable apartment with natural wood floors and high ceilings in Manhattan's NoHo neighborhood. Even though we sat around the kitchen table, there was no food or drink on offer. People referred to bullet-pointed memos and printouts. In fact, the meeting operated much like those held by businesspeople in conference rooms across the land, except for the marked absence of someone defining herself as "the boss."

Though Ross was the group's most public face, another man dominated the meeting. He had the nom de revolution of Marc and had been a Wall Street trader for twenty years; he now worked for a new company whose name he declined to share with me. He talked a blue streak and wore a porkpie hat and cufflinks. Like most bank cards of this type, a prepaid Occupy card (which at this writing remains unconnected to a bank) would allow a person to put a certain amount of money, $100 or so, on it and use it anywhere debit or credit cards were accepted. What the group earned from selling the physical cards would be used to pay for the production of the card itself and the cost of the infrastructure for its creation and administration, Marc explained.

"After all, *Occupy* Bank can't be just another bank," said Ross.

One member suggested trying another financial services company. "Cardland is a very progressive card company. We could go to them."

"The stars are aligning: so much plastic is available," said Marc, passing around a piece of paper with a full-color image of the card. It was an oceanic blue with large, round lettering: if you squinted, you might think it was a bank card from Chase. He quickly said, "It's too smooth, too corporate."

"If you put $100 on a card at CVS, you get cards for $95, which is predatory: how will ours be cheaper? We want ours to be just 99 cents," began another member of the group, absentmindedly rearranging the vitamins and the saltshaker on the tabletop.

"Why are the credit unions not dominating the card market?" a member asked.

"Credit unions are schleps," said James Sherry. "They don't have clout; they are not big enough and have no universal service." He glanced over at his wife, quietly chopping cucumbers for dinner in the corner.

Members focused not just on the details of the card but on how their still-illusory bank would be run. Ross said that the people who use the bank *are* the bank. They should decide how it operates.

"People know it; they are interested in Occupy. Those scenes in Zuccotti Park—" said one member.

"Unless we set something up, we will become a footnote," Sherry interrupted. "The card should be out in a few months." He later told me that while the group enjoyed "street cred" from the Occupy name, it was already on the wane. At the meeting, he was sharper: "The name Occupy is a wasting asset."

Like most of their meetings, this one began and ended promptly. "In this group, we don't hang," Sherry told me. "We work a lot—the bank is going to take a year and a half to build."

The projected success of the Occupy Bank rested in part on the conceit that the Occupy label had a lot of power. In his book *Occupy Nation*, Todd Gitlin pointed out that the movement had a rebel-entrepreneurial air, where ideas and dreams were what were being pitched instead of products. "We talk a lot about entrepreneurship in America," Gitlin wrote, "but the glories go to those who make capital grow. Occupy is a different kind of entrepreneurship."

The self-sustaining Occupy communities that emerged at Zuccotti Park and other sites around the country, replete with kitchens—and, in New York City, a library of five thousand books (which wound up destroyed by the city when the site was cleared)—were attempts at collectively creating a miniature version of the world the activists shared, according to anthropologist and Occupy activist David Graeber. From the start, it aimed to be a leaderless political movement. For Ross, the movement was an awakening of sorts, going far beyond clicktivism (Web-based philanthropy or "liking" certain causes) and toward a more embodied commitment to a political enterprise that occurred in very specific physical spaces.

The Occupy Wall Street working groups, such as the one on banking, had a more particular agenda than the movement overall. The larger movement's goals were deliberately less concrete. Its renegades and advocates were less small-bore in their goals than the people in the rest of this book, who want to alter our understandings of mental illness, say, or get us to see that animal suffering is important. The planned bank card was much more specific than the aims of the other amateurs and idealists in this book.

With its quants and analysts, the alternative banking working groups were a perfect example of combining both insiders and outsiders in a single movement or action; often one person could bring both approaches to bear. Their inside-outside strategy reminded me of the Treatment Action Group (TAG), an offshoot of the group AIDS Coalition to Unleash Power (ACT UP), which sprang up in the darkest moment of the AIDS crisis.

While ACT UP was passionate and theatrical, designed for the street and the public at large, TAG visited company headquarters and the halls of Congress, wearing suits and talking to the U.S. Food and Drug Administration (FDA), chemists, doctors, and pharmaceutical corporations, trying to convince them all to accelerate drug funding, development, and testing. TAG's entire membership became amateur chemists, pharmacists, and epidemiologists. They ultimately proved crucial to making the FDA speed up drug approval and design better clinical trials, among other accomplishments. TAG was a useful comparison because it showed how a certain method of organizing, one the alternative banking groups of Occupy used heavily, can work. They called this method "the inside-outside approach." As David France, the director of the documentary history of the movement *How to Survive a Plague*, said in a television interview, "inside-outside" worked because there were "the people who were very well educated, self-educated, in the issues of science and regulation and the whole drug world . . . and then the people on the streets, the soldiers who could bring thousands of people to bear to push forward the points that were being requested and demanded by the activists on the inside." Occupy the SEC was so "inside-outside" in its strategy as well that, in an interview, a member of ACT UP and one of the founders of TAG, Peter Staley, ended up comparing the Occupy group to TAG. Composed of outsiders who had once been insiders and were devoted to learning any requisite technical language and details they did not already possess, Occupy the SEC, along with the Occupy Bank Working Group, was able to get respectful coverage from *Bloomberg Businessweek*.

"Occupy has made resistance mainstream," said Ross as we sat in his home in downtown Manhattan, his six-year-old twins dancing in circles around us. "Occupy has allowed Obama to talk about inequity." One twin, a girl, twirled near a bank of windows, holding a wand. Part of what Ross hopes alternative banking can do is to empower people at large, the mass of outsiders, "to make decisions for themselves," to innovate their identities as consumers and financial clients and break the chains of "aggregate power."

An Occupy card would enable consumers to weaken centralized power by taking business away from big banks. But the Occupy Bank group and other Occupy-affiliated groups can do only so much. Their biggest contribution is the alternative paths they can create; it's up to us to adopt them. These social rebels are creating spaces for their vision, but their impact depends on other people finding and then embracing these ideas and attending meetings. Small outsider groups can't always go virtually door-to-door to sell their new languages or ideas.

It occurred to me as I played tug-of-war with Ross's daughter that if alternative banking and some of the other working groups, such as Occupy Our Homes, end up having a longer life than the wide-scale Occupy movement, it's because they are splinters that contain all the elements that are important for success as renegade movements in the digital age. In both the housing group and the banking groups, members bear down on the concrete topics in which they have a common interest. Occupy Our Homes, for instance, concentrates on foreclosed homes, encouraging people to "stand up to their banks and fight for their homes," viewing empty, boarded-up houses as items to be negotiated for rather than surrendered.

"Banks should be in public hands. Banking has been co-opted by a small monopoly that had caused immense harm. Banks should serve us, not the other way around," Ross told me on the phone in the autumn of 2012, as the group edged closer to its dream of setting up a cooperative. By October 2012, with no general assemblies bringing the multitude together, the working groups were sometimes only tenuously linked to the broader movement. Ross and other members of the group focused exclusively on the Occupy Bank and were still meeting weekly. He said he dreamed of a bank that could be a new way of organizing the economy—and, through the economy, could help accomplish the more ambitious (and even less likely) task of reorganizing society. This specific goal of a bank card and then a bank was part of a utopian vision, a reorganized society that, according to Ross, would feature decreased centralized authority. In complex systems such as banking (and so much else), people would need to become empowered agents able to make decisions for themselves, he believed. In their small way, he and his group represent some of the effects of the outsider and of cultural artifacts intervening in mainstream culture—an early symbol of a growing movement.

Would people want prepaid cards with the emblem of a heterogeneous movement on the front rather than pictures of starlets and rappers? The Occupy bankers can only hope.

AFTERWORD

Most works of journalism are self-portraits, whether their authors admit it or not. Whether written by the coldest, most calculating hacks or the most earnest reporters, such books are often hidden autobiographies: a self becomes visible if you read carefully enough. So I must acknowledge this book reflects some of my own background. My bohemian family watched avant-garde films in their friends' lofts and my mother was making her own pottery and my clothes years before the events I describe here. But it also reveals my own personal fear and fascination when, as a trained journalist working in the first decade of a new century, I first felt the encroachment of media amateurs and outsiders. I had always dreamed of being a professional literary journalist, my paragraphs glossed to high shine by editors for books and magazines. As a young adult I lived on a steady diet of 1970s journalism, sure that there was an art of the fact, that I would be paid to write it, that I would go to graduate school, and that year by year I would become more expert at it.

By 2007, though, the stakes and structures of journalism had significantly changed. All of a sudden, bloggers and vloggers were seemingly everywhere, working for free. The transformation felt as though journalism itself, my parent, was disappearing, not just my paycheck. Newspapers started to compete against the blogs and the cable news shows, which tended to be more personal or more unruly. The journalism I had aspired to create—heavily reported and long-form—seemed to have been undone by the Web's amateurs, splintering into many smaller bits of media with a lower-case *m*. My friends who wrote nonfiction fretted about where, whether offline or online, they could now publish graceful long stories about serious things and actually get paid a living wage to do so. To get painstaking reporting right takes money, time, and training. What would happen to such work in the future? We were in a jumbled zone: high- or middlebrow journalism culture, embodied by fancy journals and national newsweeklies, now hired or utilized outsider culture, such as unaffiliated bloggers, to take on those people's aura of relevance and popularity.

But over the last five years, I started to embrace the potential as well as the power of this new army of reporter-bloggers. I lost my defensiveness and started to love the amateurs. Soon high-quality long and short books by journalists were being self-published online or for the tablet. New small boutique publishers for the iPad emerged—I started working for one, in fact. A broader range of voices were getting published online, leaving behind the book manufacturing plants—and sometimes also the agents, lawyers, and publishers.

As a journalist shuttling from a world of gatekeepers into much more complicated and motley territory, I found that at least some of the millions of amateurs now writing possessed qualities that Vladimir Nabokov had used to describe great fiction: "magic, story, lesson." I started to look further afield at all the outsiders and amateurs changing other disciplines and identities. Who were they and what were they able to transform? What were their tools, and what could I, and others, learn from them?

The people in this book have turned their disabilities, limitations, or seemingly marginal positions into strengths. Living in the digital age has helped them do so. The Internet has supported people who tend to go to extremes to express themselves. It has allowed them to reach those who would otherwise be far beyond their grasp. They may become more wholly themselves in the process. The renegades in these pages, from the filmmakers and crafters to the alternative bankers and Mad Priders, are all examples of what the philosopher John Dewey called "free intelligence." Dewey thought that free intelligence, a kind of hive mind or crowdsourcing, would occur when masses of people engaged in cooperative thought. He believed that, if encouraged to flourish, these groups, which were organized not by a trained or expert elite but by the people themselves, would contribute vastly to knowledge and social change. In the past ten years, "free intelligence" is clearly on the rise. The people in this book are evidence of it and have relied on self-organization or autodidacticism rather than established top-down systems or sources.

Optimists glory in the self-organized communicative culture that brings us countless homemade films, microindependent music labels, crafters who share their skills through videos, and blog communities of everyone from the parents of gender-variant children to trans feminists. They see value in sheer abundance.

Pessimists worry about the lack of filters. I fall somewhere in the middle: I believe that there is something fundamentally virtuous in being part of a self-organized community, but I also value and cherish certain traditions and expertise.

After I learned to love the outsiders in my own field, I wondered how we all could become a little more like them. How could the rest of us join self-created communities that spring up outside or around the dictates of government, global corporations, and the other institutions that seem to rule our lives? What lessons could we learn from the people in this book as we try to locate more independent, wayward, or even more expressive parts of ourselves? And how can these groups avoid the darker side of co-optation, burning out or making innovative identities that end up lasting only a nanosecond?

My years of reporting this book also showed me something else: that while the increased power of technology can make outsiders' messages more visible, renegades and mavericks still have to make sure that what they say is sharp, refined, and inclusive. If they don't, reaching all those new eyeballs is useless: their life cycles in the public eye will be short and ineffectual.

What makes an effective rebel? For one thing, they—we—can't allow our fetish for technology- or Web-enabled visibility to act as a stand-in for real engagement or activity that leads to actual transformation. With the aid of the Web, rebels may assume people will read them or about them. But visibility equals effectiveness only if an outsider group's message is distinct, concrete, and singular. Technology is not a form of resistance unto itself; it can often be a tool for passivity as much as anything. We need to be aware that while networked communication gives new access and impact to microcultures, it can also prevent politicization by making our participation more shallow and fleeting. We may think a post, a click-through, or a "like" is a good enough expression of support for identity innovation or subversion. But it simply isn't.

The strongest renegade groups also create a clear and sometimes new language to frame and advance their renegade identities—think *Mad Pride, gender-fluid, neurodiverse, nonhuman animals,* or *Occupy banking.* The imagination and memorability of any group's language is the key to its identity innovation and to the spread of its ideas and practices to a wider public (making it, paradoxically, a little less cutting-edge due to increased familiarity).

Finally, it's crucial that renegades bolster their sense of solidarity with one another if they are to be effective. That solidarity is intensified when we meet not just online but in person. Part of what can be created by such solidarity are concentrated goals: the more particular and concrete the aims, the more effective these mavericks can be. Having clear, practical aims has made autism activists and vegans more effective, but in order to develop them, these groups had to establish an internal coherence based on affinities and commonalities. What I have found in my reporting is that the more defined the topics or issues people gather around, the more successful the outcome.

The straitjacket of cultural norms doesn't restrain the people in this book, who have found creative and sometimes somewhat perverse ways to wriggle free of these limits and thus create new modes of existence. Their practices may help form the substance of their identities as they try to create continuities between their quest for "authentic" selves and their search for a community, between something as rough and personal as craft culture and as global and efficient as mass production.

Renegades naturally look for the spaces in our culture that the mainstream has neglected or underserved and camp out there. In the process, they may sell out, going too far in their acceptance of certain aspects of the reigning modus operandi in order to get power, visibility, or the remuneration they feel they deserve. Celebrating Instagram-ready urban farms can be great, but it doesn't always lead to policy changes around industrial farming. When we rebel and resist, we must always remain mindful about the risks of co-optation—which today sometimes seems like an arcane preoccupation—while also valuing the new levels of access to the mainstream we now possess.

While there may be more and more groups supporting gender-variant youth, a transgender-inclusive civil rights bill still hasn't passed, and by 2013 we were standing on the precipice of a political and legal attack on women's reproductive rights. Michigan had placed new restrictions on safe abortion care, for instance; at the end of 2012, the Senate passed three bills that would limit abortion care, and the House is expected to consider them. I spent days at the last abortion clinic in Mississippi: the governor and state politicians were trying to shut it down, flouting the Constitution. Politicians make alarmingly frequent statements that undermine everything from the suffering of rape victims to the wage gap, dispelling any illusions I might have held about how much attitudes toward gender rights had gotten more progressive.

At the same time, more and more Americans are both relying on themselves and looking to one another as sources of information, entertainment, and assistance rather than depending upon the institutions that have too often failed us. By turning to the outside and the edges of culture, we can see a new establishment on the horizon. Sure, in some ways these groups and individuals ultimately may reproduce some of our now-existing structures and institutions, with all of their limitations. By coming to understand these small, self-regulating groups that celebrate the strangeness of the maverick, we may even perhaps retrieve parts of ourselves that our market-driven country can obscure and even obliterate. The republic of outsiders shows us that we are more than our money and that we cannot be entirely rendered into a sellable cliché—that creating obstinate, unusual identities for ourselves is more than possible. Their tools are now in all of our hands.

ACKNOWLEDGMENTS

Thanks to my many friends and colleagues for their help on this volume, a labor of love and struggle. So I must single out some particularly helpful friends and comrades: Maia Szalavitz, John Timpane, Gary Rivlin, Astra Taylor, Ann Peters, Deborah Siegel, Jennifer Dworkin, Rachel Lehmann-Haupt, Anne Kornhauser, Devorah Baum, and Dale Maharidge.

Thanks to Jesse Thiessen, Cris Beam, and Melanie Jackson. Thanks to Blue Mountain and the Nieman Foundation for giving me safe harbor. Thanks to Andrea Jones for her additional fact-checking. Thanks to Aram Sinnreich for his thoughts, Eleana Kim for her committed and rigorous thinking on this subject, as well as Laura Secor and Zephyr Teachout. Thanks to my razor-sharp mother, Barbara Quart, for additional edits, summoning not only her earlier life as a professor but an even earlier one at a publishing house. Thank you, Sarah Safer, Jeff Howe, Rachel Urkowitz, Brennan Cavanaugh, Justin Lane, Susan Lehman, Eric Alterman, Patti Cohen, Michael Massing, Martha Bebinger, Jeb Sharp, Lisa Dierbeck, Lauren Sandler, Alysia Abbott, Courtney Martin, Jess Bruder, Pagan Kennedy,

David Bornstein, Deb Amos, Ernie Beck, Richard Kaye, and The Invisible Institute. And thanks to the brilliant Sarah Fan, the most intelligent editor ever, as well as The New Press team, including Maury Botton, Sharon Swados, and Beverly Rivero. Kudos also to graphic nonfiction artist Josh Neufeld for his clever cover illustration.

Finally, I'd like to thank my daughter, Cleo, who I hope will understand some day in the future the writer's life; and my inimitable, gifted, and deeply committed husband, Peter Maass, who went over many drafts as well and showed what better or worse really meant. Finally, I'd like to thank the many renegades in this book for opening their lives and minds to me.

PUBLISHING IN
THE PUBLIC INTEREST

T hank you for reading this book published by The New Press. The New Press is a nonprofit, public interest publisher. New Press books and authors play a crucial role in sparking conversations about the key political and social issues of our day.

We hope you enjoyed this book and that you will stay in touch with The New Press. Here are a few ways to stay up to date with our books, events, and the issues we cover:

- Sign up at www.thenewpress.com/subscribe to receive updates on New Press authors and issues and to be notified about local events
- Like us on Facebook: www.facebook.com/newpressbooks
- Follow us on Twitter: www.twitter.com/thenewpress

Please consider buying New Press books for yourself; for friends and family; or to donate to schools, libraries, community centers, prison libraries, and other organizations involved with the issues our authors write about.

The New Press is a 501(c)(3) nonprofit organization. You can also support our work with a tax-deductible gift by visiting www.thenewpress.com/donate.